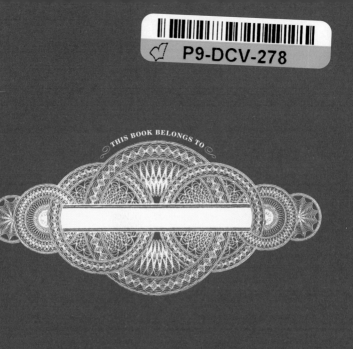

THIS BOOK BELONGS TO

PENNY
SAVING
HOUSEHOLD
HELPER

FIVE HUNDRED LITTLE WAYS

PENNY
SAVING
HOUSEHOLD
HELPER

TO SAVE BIG

By Rebecca DiLiberto

CHRONICLE BOOKS
SAN FRANCISCO

Library of Congress Cataloging-in-Publication Data available.

ISBN: 978-0-8118-7021-4

Manufactured in China

Designed by Andrew Schapiro
Typeset by Michelle Mercer and DC Type
Typeset in Excelsior, Trade Gothic, and Numbers

10 9 8 7 6 5 4 3 2 1

Chronicle Books LLC
680 Second Street
San Francisco, California 94107
www.chroniclebooks.com

To my Grandma Rosie,
who sold penny bagels around her neck as a toddler,

and my Grandpa Roff,
who ate chicken every Sunday . . . some Sundays.

TABLE OF
CONTENTS

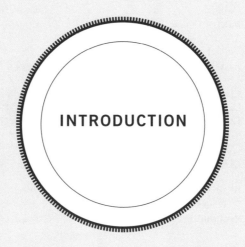

INTRODUCTION

A nyone who knows me would say I'm the last per-son they'd expect to compile a book of money-saving tips. Simply put, I love to spend money. Ever since I was old enough to read a menu, I've gotten a kick out of ordering the most expensive item on it. I think that paying a couple hundred bucks extra for a hotel room with an Olympic-sized bathtub and high-thread-count sheets is totally worth it. Send me into a clothing or shoe store, and I guarantee you I'll gravitate toward the priciest item without so much as glancing at its price tag.

But, like many of us these days, I recently came to terms with the fact that I can't go on living like this. Both my credit balance and my closet are full to bursting. My wallet is bloated with receipts. I throw away as much food as I use, and many of my magazine subscriptions go straight from the mailbox into the recycling bin.

My car might as well be permanently tethered to the gas pump. More than once, I've bought new socks and underwear because I didn't feel like doing laundry.

Because I've written for years about fashion, beauty, home decor, and celebrities, I've been exposed—and subsequently addicted—to scores of exquisite items and customs, from hundred-dollar home fragrances to ten-dollar chocolate bars; thousand-dollar spa days to ten-course prix fixe dinners. (Please note that I am by no means a millionaire—when I write about luxuries such as these, someone else is paying for them.) So, after spending plenty of time feeling ashamed by my out-of-control spending habits, I decided to find a new way to do things.

These days, no one can afford to live the way they used to. When you can barely make your house payment— if you're lucky enough to own real estate in the first place—it's pretty hard to justify taking a vacation. But who doesn't deserve a vacation—literal or metaphorical—especially in hard times like these? When the economy changed, I knew I needed to stop behaving as though I were rich. But I didn't want to stop feeling that way. So I searched for ways to maintain the comfortable—even luxurious—lifestyle I'd become accustomed to, while cutting my spending significantly.

I looked all over for insight. I pored through hundreds of mid-twentieth-century housekeeping books that were languishing in my neighborhood one-dollar book-store. I spoke to my grandparents, who lived through the Great Depression and managed to raise two impec-cably dressed, well-fed children on a modest, working-class income. I consulted all the best cooks I know, the most obsessive housecleaners, a variety of women with "World's Best Mom" mugs, and the cheapest—ahem, most frugal—people in my life.

What I learned is that luxury has more to do with your state of mind than the amount of money you spend. And I found that streamlining your life will paradoxi-cally save you money while making your surroundings feel nothing less than abundant—because you'll finally see the value of what you have.

While all the tips I list in this book will save you money, some will have a more immediate effect on your pocket-book than others.

A great deal of information here focuses on how to make everything you buy last as long as possible, and how to keep your belongings in their optimal condition. We've become so accustomed to living in a disposable society that just not throwing things away can seem like winning the lottery: when you don't throw things away, you no longer need to spend money replacing them.

I also investigated where it makes sense to spend money and where it makes more sense to save. In general, I learned that marketing adds a high markup to the price of brand-name items, and that if you're willing to go with generic or less-advertised brands, you can save a bundle without compromising on quality. And, by investing smartly in certain things that really stand out, you can create the illusion that you tolerate nothing but the best.

These days, it seems there's a specialized product for everything. We buy one scrub to clean the grout in our shower, and a different one for our kitchen sink. The bleach we throw in with the sheets barely resembles the kind we use to clean the tile—but their effects are the same. I discovered scores of different ways to use the most basic cleaning supplies, so you can reduce the number of specialized products you're buying and make the most of what you already have in your arsenal.

I was stunned to discover the magical powers of some common household items. Did you know raw potato is the MacGyver of veggies—you won't believe how many useful forms it can shapeshift into!—or that vinegar can stop time? Using humble items such as these to their fullest capacity won't just save you money—it'll also inject a little bit of magic into your daily routine.

Finally, I learned how much can be gained—both finan-cially and spiritually—from making or doing, instead of buying or shopping. The best cupcakes in the world don't need to cost $3 each—they can come right out of your kitchen for pennies. A walk through a botanical garden offers more eye candy and less temptation than a stroll around the mall. And the broth that comes out of all those chicken bones and stale veggies you used to throw away? It tastes absolutely delicious. Who knew I'd consider a second career teaching home ec?

—*Rebecca DiLiberto*

IN THE KITCHEN

COOKING

MEAT & POULTRY

1. Buy the whole chicken instead of parts. When you buy choice cuts, you pay more for the labor of cutting them up. Instead, buy whole chickens and save unused pieces for later use. And don't forget to save the bones to make a delicious savory broth.

HOW TO CUT UP A CHICKEN

For years I avoided buying a whole bird because I had no idea how to cut it into pieces. Then a butcher told me about the following easy steps: First, separate the legs from the body. Next, separate the drumsticks from the thighs. Then, separate the wings from the body. Place the chicken breast-side down and cut along each side of the spine to remove the backbone (save the backbone for stock). Finally, cut the breast in half.

2. Don't be afraid to ask your butcher for any leftover bones or trimmings when you're buying meat. You can use them to make flavorful stock to use in your cooking.

KEEPING STOCK

Take a cue from Depression-era housewives—never throw away a bone of any kind! Boil them up to make broth—add onions, carrots, celery, parsnip, and whatever other elderly veggies are taking up space in your kitchen—and pop it in the freezer to use later. It's hard to find a gourmet recipe that doesn't call for chicken, beef, or vegetable stock. This rich, slowly simmered broth adds depth to meat, pasta, and side dishes and can be used as a base for soups and gravies. Before I realized how easy it is to make, I used canned stock whenever I needed it; however, while canned stock is convenient, it's expensive, and it contains a lot of sodium. Since I also like to use organic ingredients whenever possible, and I can't be sure of the quality of the meat and veggies used to make store-bought stock, I now prefer to make my own.

STOCK CONSISTS OF THREE BASIC ELEMENTS:

• <u>Protein, fat, and gelatin</u>—found in the bones and skin of meat or fish. Vegetable stocks don't have this element, so they rely on the second two elements.

• <u>Vegetables</u>—for sweetness and depth. Root vegetables such as carrots and parsnips are classic stock ingredients, as are onions, garlic, and celery. Many chefs refer to mirepoix—carrots, onions, and celery—as the holy trinity of vegetables in French cooking, and as crucial to a good stock.

- <u>Flavorings</u>—herbs, spices, salt, and pepper. Although it is the smallest component in volume, this third element packs a big punch. It is also completely optional. Protein and vegetables are sufficient to make the most basic, and most versatile, stock.

Chicken stock is a classic, and it can be used in a mind-boggling number of recipes. It's also ridiculously easy to make. My mother, an accomplished cook, always has a pot going on her stove and it releases a delicious, fragrant aroma all over the house.

When you ask "real" cooks for their stock recipe, they'll usually laugh and say, "Recipe?" The whole point of stock is to thriftily use scraps of leftover meat and vegetables to create something out of nothing. That being said, it can be daunting to just throw a bunch of stuff in a pot with no idea of how it's going to come out. So here, provided by my mom (and vetted by the pros), is the formula for an easy stock.

Take a big stockpot—tall is better than wide, so you don't get too much evaporation—and fill it three-quarters of the way full with raw chicken bones and meat scraps. It's important to use bones—and not just meat—because the rich flavor and gelatin in the stock will come from the bone marrow. The best parts

of the chicken to use in stock are the boniest—backs, necks, wings. A good rule of thumb is to go for a ratio of 1 part bones to 1 part meat. Crack the bones before simmering them in order to release the marrow into the broth. Add enough water to cover the bones, plus 1 inch (2.5 cm). Bring to a boil.

Once it's almost boiling, reduce the heat and add the vegetables. (You don't want to boil stock, just simmer it. It's the slow cooking that produces the rich flavor.) My mom uses 2 carrots, 2 parsnips, 2 celery ribs, 2 cloves of garlic, and an onion cut in quarters as her stock staples. There's no need to peel them, because you're going to be straining the broth. You can also add any herbs or seasonings you like—fresh peppercorns, parsley, oregano, a seasoning mix—just be sure not to add anything with too much salt, since the stock will reduce and flavors will become concentrated. Most experienced cooks say that adding a bay leaf is crucial. Simmer this mixture for 2 hours, skimming the surface frequently with a big flat spoon to remove impurities. You want it to look as clear as possible. Cool the mixture, and pour it through cheesecloth to strain; then place it in the refrigerator for a couple of hours. A layer of fat will form on the surface, and this should be removed before use.

BELOW ARE A FEW VARIATIONS:

• If you want an Asian-flavored stock, add a big piece of fresh, unpeeled ginger and a bunch of scallions to the mix. Duck works really well with these ingredients.

• The French always add a bouquet garni—a flavorful pouch of herbs such as thyme, parsley, and bay leaf—to their stock. You can buy this in an expensive gourmet store, but it's much cheaper and easier to make your own using your favorite herbs. Just bind them together using butcher twine and wrap in cheesecloth. You can even throw them in a tea strainer for easy removal.

• The technique for making fish stock is the same as the one for chicken, but the fish you choose is really important—avoid anything oily like salmon. Leeks and fennel added to the vegetable mix will complement the fish's flavor, as will white wine added to the water. And, although fish heads can look a little scary, many top chefs say that they make the best stock.

• There's a key difference between making beef stock and chicken stock: though chicken bones can be dropped right into the stockpot raw, roasting beef bones, meat, and fat before simmering them will create a deeper flavor. It will also enable you to discard some fat before putting the meat into the pot.

FINALLY, HERE ARE A FEW TIPS
FOR MAKING STOCK:

• Cooked bones and scraps from a big holiday turkey are ideal for making your stock. Just don't under-season. You might have added plenty of herbs and spices when you roasted the turkey, but you still need to add seasonings when you're making stock from its carcass. Cloves, peppercorns, thyme, and parsley create a rich, festive taste when added to the seasoning mix.

• Although some people consider it cheating, adding a bouillon cube or two to your stock is a quick and easy way to give it lots of flavor, especially if you don't have time to simmer it slowly for hours. Make sure the brand you choose contains no MSG, and, since bouillon is mostly salt, don't add extra salt without tasting first.

• For your next dinner party, consider serving your stock as a wonderfully retro first course, with a crouton and a sprig of parsley floating on top. You'll want to make your stock crystal clear, though, before presenting it with such flair. Here's a trick for making a truly clear stock: After you've strained the stock, chilled it, and skimmed off the hardened fat, put the clarified stock back on the stove and bring to a simmer (this is the stage that comes just before a low boil—when a bubble or two appears every couple of seconds). For every 1 cup (240 ml) of stock you're clarifying, put one egg white in a bowl. Save the eggshells. Beat the egg whites and crush the shells, then add both to the simmering stock. Boil for 5 minutes and strain the liquid through cheesecloth.

TEN WAYS TO USE YOUR STOCK:

1. As a base for noodle soup (Just add leftover meat, noodles, and diced veggies.)
2. As a basting liquid for your holiday turkey
3. Instead of water in your rice or cooked grains
4. As a base for sauces and gravies

5. Instead of sautéeing in oil or butter, steam meats and veggies in stock to make your favorite recipes low-fat.
6. As a steaming liquid for vegetables
7. As a poaching liquid for chicken or fish
8. To moisten your holiday stuffing
9. As the best cold medicine in the world
10. To reintroduce lost moisture to reheated leftovers

3. To keep protein structure intact and preserve flavor, avoid salting meat before you freeze it. Salt speeds up the process that causes meat to spoil, so cured meats like bacon and ham should be used within a month of freezing. Hot dogs and cold cuts, because of the way they're preserved, should not be frozen. Also, to maximize freshness, do not store meat in grocery store wrapping—rewrap it yourself so air pockets don't cause freezer burn.

4. Meat tends to be the most expensive food item at the grocery store. Use less meat—and sneak more veggies into your family's diet—by stuffing veggies such as peppers, cabbage, and mushrooms with a mixture of ground meat or poultry, aromatic vegetables, and breadcrumbs. Try putting a mixture of ground beef, rice, tomatoes, and your favorite seasoning into bell peppers, or try stuffing cabbage leaves with ground turkey, sautéed onions, and garlic, and then baking them until cooked thoroughly.

5. Chopped meat spoils more quickly than whole cuts do, so use your chopped meats immediately or freeze them as soon as possible after purchase.

6. Less expensive cuts of meat tend to be tougher than more expensive cuts. You might consider using a traditional meat-tenderizing mallet on tougher cuts, but this can result in thin cutlets that may not be suited for your recipe. Instead, try gently scoring the surface of the meat with a pizza cutter. The shallow scores created by the pizza cutter will make meat surprisingly tender.

7. Marinate inexpensive cuts of meat in a mixture that contains at least one of the following: tomatoes, citrus juice, vinegar, papaya, pineapple, or beer. All contain enzymes that combat toughness. Then, slow roast.

8. With the rising cost of high-quality meat, a pound of hamburger never seems to go far enough. Try mixing a few handfuls of crushed cereal or bread crumbs into your hamburger to make it go further.

FISH

9. Getting all the omega-3 fatty acids that fish provides can be pretty pricey. An inexpensive and delicious solution is to incorporate canned anchovies into your cooking. They're rich in healthful fats, and they add a savory taste to salad dressings, pastas, and pizzas. If the look of these hairy little fish turns you off, sauté them in olive oil and garlic before using—they'll dissolve into an olive-like relish. Or buy anchovy paste, which virtually disappears into sauces and salad dressings.

10. Buy frozen. Fish that's flash frozen is of the same quality as fresh fish—restaurants use it all the time.

11. Ask the fishmonger at your local grocery store about upcoming sales.

12. For the freshest catch, shop your local fish or farmers' markets.

DAIRY & EGGS

13. Save those cheese rinds. The rind of hard cheese adds a rich flavor to soup stock. Just add the rind when you're simmering the stock; then remove the rind and strain the broth.

14. If you are not sure whether an egg is fresh, don't throw it out right away. Instead, see how it behaves in a cup of water. Bad eggs float; fresh ones sink.

15. When a recipe calls for whites only, you don't need to waste the yolks. Instead of cracking the egg in half, cut a small hole in one end of the shell to let the white drain out. Then seal the hole with a piece of tape, wrap the eggshell in foil, and refrigerate. You can also store egg yolks out of their shells in a cup of cold water so they stay separate and keep their shape. Cover them with plastic and store in the fridge. Both these methods keep yolks fresh for up to 5 days.

16. Shelled egg whites also keep in the fridge for a week, and there's no need to suspend them in water—just put them in a plastic bag or in a ramekin covered with plastic wrap.

17. Egg cartons are the best containers for keeping eggs fresh. Keep eggs in their original packaging until you use them—and make sure their larger ends face up.

18. Don't throw away your butter wrappers once the stick is gone; fold them up, store them in the fridge, and use them the next time you need to grease a baking pan. You can also use them before you sauté—just warm the skillet and wipe it down with the wrapper. The butter will melt right off.

19. If you store your cheese wrapped in a kitchen towel or a piece of cheesecloth dampened with vinegar, it won't dry out. A bonus: the vinegar impedes mold growth and won't affect the cheese's taste.

20. You can also keep your cheese from drying out by spreading butter or margarine on the cut sides so no moisture can escape. This works best with hard cheeses partially sealed in wax.

21. Another way to prevent mold is to wrap a few sugar cubes in with your cheese. The sugar will absorb moisture.

22. In order to make your cottage cheese or sour cream last longer, store it upside down in the fridge in its original container. Because inverting the container creates a vacuum, spoilage-creating bacteria grow more slowly.

23. Most people don't know that cheese can be frozen. If your guests don't polish off that triple crème, put it back in its original package, wrap tightly in plastic, and freeze. Soft cheeses with a high fat content freeze best. Defrost the cheese slowly in the fridge a day before you plan to serve it again.

24. To guard against food spoilage should your power go out, keep a couple of plastic bottles three-quarters full of water in your freezer. If you move these to the fridge when your electricity goes out, they will keep the food in your fridge cold until the power comes back on. They also make great ice packs for coolers and, because they take up space, they will keep your freezer running more efficiently.

25. Some say that a pinch of baking soda magically sends sour milk back in time—just add 2 teaspoons of baking soda for every 1 cup (240 ml) of milk. For those who are put off by the idea of chugging uncooked milk that's past its prime, sour milk is a boon in recipes for pancake batter or fried chicken. Just use it as you would buttermilk.

26. If you burn milk when heating it on the stove, add a pinch of salt to take away the scorched smell and taste.

27. When cheese dries out, don't throw it away. Instead, grate it over pasta, vegetables, or soup—anything with a high moisture content.

28. Stock up on butter when it's on sale—you can store it in the freezer for up to 6 months. Just make sure you pack it in an airtight container, so it doesn't take on the flavor of whatever else you're keeping in there.

29. Next time milk is on sale and you have some room in your freezer, buy several gallons. You can freeze milk without affecting its taste or quality for up to 3 months. When you're ready to use it, thaw in the refrigerator for 12 hours, and then shake to counteract any separation.

30. You can use evaporated milk in any recipe that calls for whipping cream—even if you need it to be fluffy when whipped. Just chill the evaporated milk the same way you'd chill the cream, and use an electric beater to make it stand up.

PASTA, RICE & POTATOES

31. A bay leaf slipped into a container of flour, pasta, or rice will help to keep bugs away.

32. To keep it from hardening, store left-over cooked pasta in a sealed plastic bag and refrigerate. When you are ready to serve it, take a tip from chefs and throw it in boiling water for just a few seconds to heat and restore its moisture balance.

33. Have leftover rice? You have many options here. Make it into rice pudding by adding butter, cinnamon, sugar, and milk. Create authentic fried rice by sautéing with a beaten egg, soy sauce, sliced green onions, and mushrooms. Add to stock for a simple soup kids will love. Toss in slivered almonds and raisins for a Middle Eastern–inspired pilaf.

34. Baked or boiled potatoes cook and brown quickly, making for excellent hash browns. Throw some butter or olive oil in a pan and sauté cooked potato slices or chunks. Crush potatoes and add sliced green onions for home fries, or keep potato slices intact for a fancier dinnertime side.

35. Who hasn't burned rice five minutes before dinnertime? Rather than cooking a new batch—and wasting more rice—put a slice of bread on top of the charred rice and replace the lid on the pan. Let it stand for 10 minutes while the bread absorbs the burned flavor. Then spoon out the unscorched rice.

BREADS, MUFFINS & CRACKERS

36. Some people say that placing a stalk of celery in a bag of bread will keep it fresh. Though many old-school homemakers seem to know this tip, no one has been able to explain why it works. My guess is that since celery has an extremely high moisture content, it keeps the bread from drying out.

37. To keep your crackers extra fresh and crisp, store them in the bottom drawer of your gas oven. The heat from the pilot light will prevent them from going stale. Be sure to keep the crackers in their original packaging, not a plastic container—and, of course, take them out before you use the oven or broiler.

38. Rather than storing extra pancake or waffle batter in the fridge, where you may forget to use it, cook those last few pancakes or waffles, package them in single servings, and freeze. When you need a quick breakfast, just reheat the frozen waffles or pancakes in the toaster oven. Book-ending a fried egg and slice of cheese, they make an excellent breakfast sandwich.

39. No need to snub day-old muffins at the bakery—or in your own kitchen. Sprinkle them with water, place them in a paper bag, and put them in a hot oven for 5 to 10 minutes. The steam created by the water will restore their moisture.

40. If you burn a loaf of bread, don't throw it away—grate the top off with a cheese grater. If the lighter-colored patch on the crust bothers you, brown it under the broiler for a sec—just don't burn it again!

41. When crackers, pretzels, or chips have gone stale, revive them by spreading them out in a single layer on a jelly-roll pan or cookie sheet and broiling for a minute.

WHAT TO DO WITH YOUR STALE BREAD
(IT'S GOOD FOR MORE THAN TRIPS TO THE DUCK POND.)

Revive it. Put in a 300°F (150°C / gas 2) oven for 10 minutes.

Make toast. Day-old bread makes better toast than fresh bread does, since it contains less moisture.

Make hors d'oeuvres. Cut the stale bread into small rounds and freeze. Then toast the rounds to make a cheap and handy substitute for fancy crackers.

Make croutons. Cut the bread into ½-inch (1.2-cm) cubes; drizzle olive oil on top; sprinkle on garlic powder, salt, and pepper; and bake at 325°F (180°C/gas 4) for 15 minutes. It's best to use these croutons right after you make them or they could become too chewy.

Make bread crumbs. Leftover white bread—dried out, but not moldy—makes excellent bread crumbs. Slice the bread and throw it in a 300°F (150°C/gas 2) oven for 10 minutes to dry it out. Break up hard slices and pulse them in a food processor until they've become the texture of lumpy sand. (You can also crush the bread in a sealed plastic bag if you don't have a food processor.) Store crumbs in airtight plastic bags in the freezer.

> HERE ARE SOME WAYS TO USE YOUR BREAD CRUMBS:
> • Sprinkle over the top of your baked macaroni and cheese for a crunchy topping.
>
> • Mix with ground meat to make meatloaf or meatballs.

• Mix in some grated cheese, oregano, salt, and pepper and use as a coating for pan-frying chicken or eggplant Italian style. Just beat an egg, dip your chicken breast or sliced eggplant in it, and dredge in the crumbs. Heat some canola oil (it's cheaper than olive, and it has a higher smoking point) in a sauté pan, and fry until golden brown. Serve with fresh lemon wedges or tomato sauce. Or melt mozzarella over the golden cutlets for a quick parmigiana.

• Mix with chopped mushrooms, Parmesan cheese, and parsley and use the mixture to stuff mushroom caps as an appetizer or side dish.

• Sprinkle over halved tomatoes, dot with butter, and broil for a steakhouse-style side.

• Toast in a pan with garlic, olive oil, and pancetta (Italian bacon) and toss with buttered spaghetti.

• Make *arancini*, Italian rice balls that make a delicious appetizer. Just mix 2 cups (430 g) of leftover risotto with 2 eggs, a half cup (60 g) of grated cheese, and ¾ cup (80 g) of bread crumbs. Form into little balls, coat with more bread crumbs, and fry in vegetable oil until golden brown. Serve with a side of marinara sauce for dipping.

• Form cold, leftover mashed potatoes into little balls, dip in beaten egg, coat in bread crumbs, and sauté or deep-fry for easy croquettes. You can also mix in some leftover crabmeat, salmon, or turkey for an easy, fancy appetizer.

- Make a quick and easy quiche crust. Spread a pie plate with soft butter, then press toasted bread crumbs into the butter to form a tightly packed, uniform layer. Freeze until set, then add quiche mixture, and bake.

- Mix with brown sugar, cinnamon, and chopped nuts and sprinkle over stone fruit for a quick brown Betty. Bake until bubbling, and serve with ice cream.

Make bread pudding. Whether sweet or savory, warm bread pudding is at the top of most people's list of comfort foods. Stale bread, because of its reduced moisture content, makes better bread pudding than fresh does. Serve your pudding as a dessert or a side dish.

Here is my basic recipe for bread pudding: Beat together 2 cups (480 ml) milk, 4 large eggs, and ½ cup (100 g) sugar. Spread ½ pound (200 g) stale bread, cut into 1-inch (2.5-cm) cubes, into a buttered 9-by-9-inch (23-by-23-cm) square baking pan. Pour the milk-and-egg mixture (the custard) over the bread and bake in a 350°F (180°C/gas 4) oven until it's golden brown. (Some richer recipes call for more yolks than whites and cream instead of milk, but I prefer this lighter version.) The dish's flavor and personality will come from whatever extras you add to these basics.

BREAD PUDDING VARIATIONS:
- Baguette with heirloom tomatoes, Parmesan cheese, and basil. Cut 1 pound (455 g) of heirloom tomatoes and a tablespoon of chopped fresh basil into the bread

mixture. Sprinkle with 3 ounces (90 g) grated Parmesan cheese, salt, and pepper. Pour custard mixture over the bread and tomatoes, and then sprinkle another ounce (30 g) of Parmesan on top.

• Chocolate croissants with overripe cherries. Add ½ cup (100 g) sugar and 1 teaspoon vanilla to the custard mix. Combine chocolate croissant chunks and pitted cherries, pour sweet custard on top, and bake.

• Levain bread (hearty, sour, and French) with wild mushrooms and Gruyére. Sauté 1 pound (455 g) sliced wild mushrooms (I like porcini and shiitake, but any kind will work) in olive oil with a clove of garlic, a shallot, and a rib of celery, all finely chopped. Salt and pepper to taste. Sprinkle 2 ounces (56 g) shredded Gruyére over the bread cubes, and pour the warm mushroom mixture on top. Add the custard, then an additional 2 ounces (56 g) of shredded Gruyére. Sprinkle generously with freshly ground black pepper before baking.

• Biscuits, raisins, and spice. Pour ½ cup (120 ml) warm milk over biscuits to soften them. Add ½ cup (85 g) raisins, 1 teaspoon cinnamon, and 1 teaspoon nutmeg. Add ¾ cup (150 g) sugar and 1 teaspoon (5 ml) vanilla to the custard mix, pour on top, and bake as usual.

Since bread pudding is sort of a kitchen-sink operation, feel free to experiment with your favorite ingredients—or whatever you have lying around—to create a dish that's all your own.

Make bread salad. I love to order bread salad because it's the ultimate dish of denial—I seem to be ordering a salad, but what I'm really ordering is a bread basket, just for myself. Bread salad is almost easier to make at home than it is to order; just combine cubed stale, toasted bread, raw veggies, and dressing. Most cultures have their own version of bread salad—here are my two favorites.

ITALIAN PANZANELLA
Combine a loaf of stale crusty bread—cut into 1-inch (2.5-cm) cubes and toasted—with 1 cup (236 ml) coarsely chopped tomatoes, 1 cup (236 g) sliced cucumber, and a sliced red onion. Mix ½ cup (120 ml) extra-virgin olive oil, 3 tablespoons red wine vinegar, 1 clove of garlic (minced), and 1 teaspoon dried oregano together with a whisk. Pour the dressing over the salad and toss. Season with salt and freshly ground pepper.

MIDDLE-EASTERN FATTOUSH SALAD
This is a great way to get rid of stale pita or flat bread. Toast the bread until it's the consistency of chips, then crumble it into large pieces. Thinly slice a small red onion and marinate in lemon juice. Chop 2 ripe tomatoes and a large cucumber and combine in a bowl with ½ cup (24 g) chopped mint and ½ cup (24 g) chopped parsley. Drain the onions and add them. Toss with ½ cup (120 ml) olive oil, the juice of 2 lemons, 1 teaspoon red wine vinegar, 1 teaspoon ground sumac, 1 crushed garlic clove, and salt and pepper to taste. Fold in pita crumbles. Top with feta cheese and/or Kalamata olives, if desired.

FATS & OILS

42. Strained through cheesecloth, and stored in an airtight container in a cool, dark place, vegetable oil can be used over and over again for deep frying until it goes rancid. To slow the rancidity process, don't mix different types of oils and don't fry in iron or copper pans. When the oil darkens, thickens, or smells "off," it should be replaced with new oil.

43. It's practically un-American to throw away your bacon fat. Store it in an airtight aluminum or stainless-steel container in the freezer, and use it to make cornbread, to fry eggs or potatoes, or instead of oil in a spinach salad dressing (try 2 parts bacon fat to 3 parts balsamic vinegar, or add 1 part vegetable oil to the mix if you like a less pungent dressing).

HERBS & SPICES

44. To keep herbs tasting fresh for up to a month, store them in whole bunches, sealed in plastic bags, in the freezer. When you need to use them, they'll be easier to chop, and they'll defrost the minute they hit a hot pan.

45. Spices can be really expensive, so it's important to use them to the last dash. Stored in a cool, dark place, they'll last up to 4 years. And there's no risk of spoiling—even if spices lose their potency due to age, they can't go bad.

DESSERTS & SWEETS

46. You don't need to invest in a fancy cookie jar; instead, store cookies in an airtight ice bucket to keep them fresh. Or, for small or round cookies, use a coffee can.

47. Store crispy and chewy cookies in separate containers. If you combine them, the moisture from the chewy cookies will make the crispy ones lose their crunch.

48. To make store-bought cake frosting go twice as far, whip it with your electric mixer and let air plump it up.

49. While you can make most baked goods ahead of time and freeze them until use, those with frostings that contain brown sugar or egg whites don't freeze well. Instead, freeze the cake alone and make the frosting fresh when you're ready to serve it. Or, if you have a leftover cake that's already frosted, cut off the frosted part and repurpose the cake by topping it with a fruit or caramel sauce when you serve it.

50. When you don't have enough juice left for a whole glass, make single popsicles. You don't need a special mold; just use a small Dixie cup (half of a wooden chopstick works as well as a popsicle stick). The stick will stand up straight if you let the juice freeze partially before inserting it.

51. To cross one item off your shopping list, stop using muffin-tin liners when you bake. Coat tins with nonstick oil spray, and baked goods will slide right out.

52. A festive dinner party calls for a fancy dessert, but who wants to drop $25 at the bakery? To save time and money, try one of the following:

- Layer vanilla ice cream with crushed cookies (or even just cookie crumbs) in a martini glass; top with a berry.

- Heat canned peaches in a saucepan, add a cinnamon stick and a shot of brandy, and simmer until it thickens. Serve over vanilla ice cream.

- Make instant chocolate pudding with whipping cream instead of water to make a rich-tasting mousse.

- Throw together a trifle with sliced grocery-store pound cake, whipped cream, and overripe berries macerated with sugar and your favorite liqueur.

FRUITS

53. When juicing citrus fruits, roll them back and forth on the counter with the palm of your hand to release their liquid from the segments inside. Extra dry or old lemons may also benefit from a quick bath in warm water or a few seconds in the microwave.

54. When you're done with a piece of citrus fruit, pop the leftover rinds into a resealable plastic bag and store them in the freezer. Then, when you're using a recipe that calls for zest (the colored outer surface of the rind), grate the zest with a cheese grater or Microplane, and throw the white pith away.

55. We all waste a good percentage of a strawberry's fruit by "cleaning" it, which to most of us means cutting its top off. To minimize waste, pull off the leaves at the top of the berry, and push a drinking straw through from top to bottom instead. The straw removes just the berry's core, leaving more fruit than a paring knife does.

56. Need a quick and delicious sweet sauce? The syrup that canned fruits swim in is delicious when heated and poured over pie or ice cream—or both!

57. When your recipe calls for just a few drops of lemon juice, don't cut the lemon in half—it will dry out quickly that way. Instead, puncture it and squeeze out just what you need. Save the rest in the fridge, wrapped in plastic.

58. Buy inexpensive, unripe fruit, and place it in a paper bag with an apple overnight. The apple will release ethylene gas that will speedily ripen the fruit.

59. Moreover, keep apples away from already ripe fruits, because the gas they let off can lead to early spoilage.

60. Don't separate your bananas from one another until you plan to eat them—they last longer in a bunch.

61. Though some people might turn their noses up at darkened bananas, they're excellent for baking. If you can't use them right away, squash them with a potato masher and freeze in plastic for later use.

62. When freezing fruit, be sure to leave enough space in the container for it to expand as it freezes.

63. Freshen dried coconut by steaming it over a pot of boiling water.

64. If you live near a family-owned farm, you may be able to save on fruit by picking your own. Picking fruit is also a great family or date activity.

VEGETABLES

65. Eat only what's in season. Not only does seasonal produce cost less, but it also tastes better. Buy it at your local farmers' market to get the highest quality and eliminate the middleman.

66. When cutting corn from the cob, I often seem to lose as many kernels as I collect. This solution is so simple it's ingenious: to minimize waste and mess, mount the cob in the hollow center of an angel food or Bundt cake pan, where it will be secure. When you run the knife down the cob, kernels will collect neatly in the pan.

67. Make use of vegetable trimmings you usu- ally throw away. Pea pods, cel- ery leaves, carrot tops, broccoli stalks—all these castaways add rich flavor to stocks, sauces, and soups.

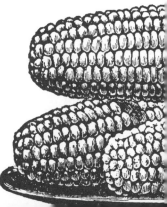

68. Line the bottom of your refrigerator's veggie drawer with paper towels. These will absorb the excess moisture that causes veggies to spoil.

69. Mushrooms are so delicate—stored in the fridge they can get slimy; at room temperature they seem to spoil or harden overnight. Control their moisture level by storing them in the refrigerator in a brown paper bag, or in paper towels.

70. Yellow beans seem to discolor the minute you get them home from the market. When this happens, don't toss them—get rid of brown spots with a 2-hour bath of 2 parts white vinegar to 1 part water.

71. Onions should be stored in a cool, dark place—but not in the refrigerator. The problem is this: tucked in a bowl touching one another, onions quickly spoil—or grow snaky green tentacles. A simple solution? Keep them in old pantyhose. Drop one onion in, tie a knot, then the next, and so on. Then you can snip off one at a time. You can either hang them or store them in a bowl this way.

72. If you have some wilted lettuce that is truly unsalvageable, use a few of the old leaves to protect fresh ones from wilting. Just use wilted leaves to wrap fresh ones, like a present. Wrap the bundle in paper towels and store in plastic wrap in the fridge.

73. Gazpacho may sound sophisticated and exotic, but it's basically leftover tomato salad blitzed in the blender. Add croutons made from stale bread, a dash of olive oil, and a few drops of red wine vinegar, and your guests will feel like they've gone to Spain.

74. Dress your salad individually at the table instead of coating it all before you serve. This way, uneaten salad won't get wilted and soggy.

75. Leftover cooked vegetables are great to have on hand to use as filling for omelets and frittatas. You can also layer them on top of tortillas and sprinkle with cheese for a quesadilla, or warm them and serve over chilled lettuce leaves with vinaigrette for a sophisticated salad.

76. Lettuce can sometimes wilt during the car ride home from the grocery store. Tossing it would be like flushing a five-dollar bill down the drain, so revive it instead. Add vinegar or lemon juice to a bowl of cold water and soak the wilted leaves in the liquid for an hour—they'll perk right up.

77. When radishes, celery, or carrots have lost their crunch, pop them in a bowl of iced water with a slice of raw potato and watch them get fresh again right before your eyes.

78. Asparagus wilts quickly if you don't use it right away. When your stalks go limp, fill a wide-mouthed drinking glass halfway with cold water, and stand the asparagus in it with the cut ends down. The stalks will respond like thirsty flowers and drink the moisture right up. This trick also works with celery and carrots.

79. Vegetables that are usually eaten raw don't do well in the freezer. To preserve them, pickle them instead.

80. Don't waste your cash on precut fruits and veggies at the grocery store. Though these can seem convenient, they can cost twice as much as whole produce. Not to mention the fact that they spoil easily and you can't be sure of their quality, or even whether they've been washed thoroughly.

PICKLING AT HOME

I love homemade pickles, but I've always found the idea of making them myself really intimidating. Canning jars? Boiling vinegar? It seems like a lot of work for something you can buy at the grocery store. But as I've become more of a pickle connoisseur, cheap unrefrigerated grocery store pickles have begun to taste like limp, overprocessed salt licks to  me. On the other hand, I just can't justify spending up to $15 per jar for artisanal pickles made in small batches—the delicious kind you buy at gourmet stores. That's why I finally broke down and tried a few easy pickling recipes. And I was amazed to see how simple the process really is. Since you keep these pickles in the refrigerator, shelf stability (and botulism!) aren't really the concerns they are with canning, so there's no fear factor. And once you learn the basic steps, you can customize the recipe to suit your tastes and your needs—pickles go way beyond dill and cukes. These sharp little guys make a snappy low-cal snack and a great accompaniment to any meal. Throw on a ribbon and a homemade label and they make tasty holiday gifts, too.

Here's my own basic pickle recipe—I say basic because it doesn't require any weird ingredients or sterilized jars, or too much effort. Don't be afraid to experiment once you get the hang of the fundamentals—you may become famous for your ginger-sesame-wasabi cornichons, or your balsamic-oregano green tomatoes. And, if you get a little too creative, don't worry if you have to toss those not-so-yummy clove, mint, and chipotle radishes—radishes come pretty cheap.

QUICKLES: MAKES 2 QUARTS (1.82 LITERS)

YOU'LL NEED:
2 pounds (910 g) Kirby cucumbers (These are sometimes called "pickling cucumbers," probably because they make such good pickles. They have tiny seeds and thin skin and really maintain their crunch—maybe because they have a lower water content than some other varieties.)

3 tablespoons coarse salt
(If a cloudy look bothers you, use pickling salt.)

3 cups (720 ml) filtered water

2 cups (480 ml) distilled white vinegar

1 tablespoon dill seeds

4 cloves peeled garlic

½ teaspoon crushed red pepper flakes
(optional—I am a spice fiend!)

2 bunches fresh dill, coarsely chopped
(or 1 bunch dill and 1 bunch fresh parsley)

TO MAKE THE QUICKLES:

1. Cut the cucumbers into circular slices ½ inch (1.2 cm) thick and toss them in a strainer. Cover with salt and mix with your hands. Set atop a bowl in the refrigerator for 1 hour to draw the excess moisture out of the cukes.

2. Rinse, drain, and pat the cucumber slices dry. Put them in a bowl and set aside.

3. Combine all the remaining ingredients—except the fresh herbs—in a saucepan, and bring to a boil. Simmer for 4 minutes; then turn off the heat and cool for 10 minutes.

4. Add the chopped dill and/or parsley to the cucumber slices. Cover with the warm brine. Let the mixture cool for at least 30 minutes, then transfer to airtight glass jars and refrigerate for at least a week. Your Quickles will be good for a month after the date of canning. (If you plan to give them as a gift, be sure to write the expiration date on the jar.)

QUICKLES VARIATIONS

You can come up with an infinite number of variations on this recipe by using different vegetables and flavorings:

Instead of cucumbers, try green beans or haricot verts, radishes, cauliflower, zucchini, baby carrots, beets . . . the list is endless. Try adding hot peppers, a teaspoon of sugar, coriander seeds (approximately 2 g), or fennel seeds (approximately 2 g) instead of dill to the vinegar mixture.

Here are some of my favorite pickles, all variations of the basic recipe on page 50:

Cauliflower with red pepper and oregano: Cut cauliflower into small florets and blanch for 1 minute before pickling (plunge them into boiling water for a minute, then plunge into ice water). Replace dill seeds with 1 teaspoon red pepper flakes and 1 tablespoon dried oregano. Replace fresh dill with chopped Italian parsley. This creates a taste reminiscent of classic Italian *giardiniera*.

Fennel with orange juice and star anise: Add the rind of 1 orange to the boiling mixture. Replace dill seeds with star anise seeds. Replace fresh dill with chopped fennel tops.

Haricot verts with wasabi and soy: Blanch haricots verts—small French green beans—for 1 minute before pickling. Replace dill seeds with ½ teaspoon dried wasabi powder and ½ teaspoon dried ginger. Replace ½ cup (120 ml) vinegar with ½ cup (120 ml) soy sauce. Use rice vinegar instead of distilled white vinegar.

Dilly radishes: Follow the cucumber recipe, replacing cucumbers with small red radishes.

COMPLETE MEALS

81. Make your own TV dinners instead of buying packaged frozen ones. They'll taste better, they'll be more healthful, and, assuming you have leftovers once in a while, they're basically free.

Just place complete, individual meals in containers with compartments—you can find disposable ones in most grocery stores, and both Tupperware and Pyrex make them as well. I like to use oven-safe ones because I try never to put plastic in my microwave. You can also freeze individual portions of soup or stew in zip-top plastic bags—just be sure to read the box the bags come in to make sure they're heat-safe—and heat them in boiling water when you're hungry.

82. Make your own packaged kids' lunch kits. In addition to costing less than the mass-produced kind, they will be more nutritious, taste better, and use much less packaging. For a pizza kit, put some shredded cheese and pepperoni slices in a baggie, and put triangles of pita bread in another, so your child can compose miniature slices. For fajitas, slice some leftover beef or chicken into thin strips, and pack with bell peppers cut to the same size, along with a tortilla. For beverages, use a thermos instead of juice boxes, or an aluminum water bottle instead of disposable plastic ones. These choices will teach your kids about conservation while saving you money.

83. Breakfast is the most important meal of the day. Luckily, it's also the cheapest. Oatmeal and eggs are nutritious, filling, and very affordable. Eat these in the morning with some fruit and you'll eat less all day long, saving you money—and calories!

COFFEE & TEA

84. When you brew a pot of coffee that nobody drinks, don't pour it down the drain. Freeze leftovers in ice cube trays to add to iced coffee instead of ice cubes. Your coffee won't lose its potency as the cubes melt.

85. Tea bags can lose their flavor once the plastic wrap is removed from the box. To preserve freshness, keep tea in an airtight container.

86. There's some controversy among coffee connoisseurs about how best to store coffee beans to maintain freshness, but it does seem that keeping them in an airtight bag—in the freezer, or in another cool, dark place—extends their life dramatically.

OTHER BEVERAGES

87. Don't waste your money on top-shelf liquor for punches and mixed drinks—it's difficult to discern the subtleties of expensive liquor when it's mixed with other ingredients. Instead, go for value when making a big batch of cocktails for a party.

88. Just say no to bottled water. In addition to being expensive, its quality is unregulated by the government, and it may contain high levels of BPA, a contaminant found in some plastics that can leech into liquids and harm your health. Invest in a water filtration system for your kitchen sink, and all the water you use will be of the highest quality—and virtually free.

89. Leftover wine can be made into vinegar— the kind that can cost up to $10 for a small bottle at the grocery store. To make it yourself, all you need is some unpasteurized vinegar—inexpensive and available at any health food store—to start the process going. The unpasteurized vinegar will help in the creation of what is called "the mother"—a living culture that turns wine into vinegar. Pour approximately 1 cup (240 ml) of the unpasteurized vinegar into a big glass jar, and add the dregs of whatever wine you have. Cover the mouth with gauze or cheesecloth and secure with a rubber band so that the mixture can "breathe." In about two weeks, you'll have a big slimy mess on the surface of the liquid. That's the mother. Save it in a sealed glass container for the next time you want to make vinegar—it's a living thing and won't spoil. The liquid underneath the mother is your homemade vinegar! Pour through cheesecloth to strain, and enjoy.

GROWING YOUR OWN

90. Hippies are not the only ones who grow their own vegetables—smart consumers who want to avoid pesticides and control their spending also invest in small plots. If you're lucky enough to have some extra land on your property, plant a vegetable garden. See if you can interest any of your friends and neighbors in doing the same in their yards—then you can swap produce and spread the wealth of zucchini, tomatoes, or any other bumper crops.

91. Plant an indoor herb "garden" by placing small pots of herbs along your kitchen windowsill. A living plant will cost roughly the same amount as one bunch of cut herbs from the grocery store, and it will produce much more in volume.

92. Grow cherry tomatoes indoors, in a flower pot. Sweet 100 seedlings work best, since their fruits are tiny.

COOKING FOR FRIENDS & FAMILY

93. If you can't grow a garden but still want to start a food swap network, create a cooking tree. Assign each person a category of food and then swap to create full meals.

START A COOKING TREE

A system that helps you share cooking costs and duties with friends and family will save you money and time. Your cooking tree can be as simple or as intricate as you like—use it to split up holiday meal duties once or twice a year, or to provide dinner relief every week.

Just recruit a group of members and meet to determine the scope and process of your cooking club, Type out a calendar with duties and contact info and distribute it to everyone involved. Publishing information on a blog is an easy way to make sure everyone has access to the most updated information. Organize things in a way that best suits the needs of your group—there's no perfect formula. Here are some ideas, though:

- Sunday night suppers: Each member makes a whole meal once a month, or one component of a complete meal every week.

- Holiday side dishes and desserts: Each member is responsible for his or her family's main course, plus one side large enough to share with everyone. Then, pre-dinner, share around the sides.

- School lunches and snacks: Make five lunches once a week instead of one lunch five times per week. Collaborate with parents in your children's school; drop the lunches off with your kid.

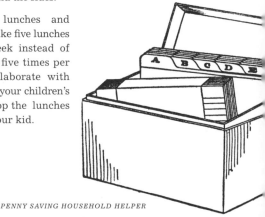

• Microwaveable diet meals: Following a set plan can require an absurd amount of cooking, but splitting up duties will definitely increase your chance of success. Share a diet book, groceries, and prep time, and gain invaluable moral support (and more time for exercising).

• Christmas cookies: Split up a giant batch into several small ones, and exchange with friends to get a variety of sweets that will last throughout the holidays.

Choose a convenient, central location for food drop-off and pickup, and be sure to pack everything in a cooler once you get to the drop-off location so it doesn't spoil in transit. Share recipes and feedback on the club blog—it will become a nice chronicle of everyone's culinary adventures throughout the year.

CHEAP DINNER PARTIES

When it comes to throwing a dinner party, I usually decide whether I am going for style or substance and then spend accordingly. If I'm having a few good friends over for a casual meal and catch-up, I like to go for good local and organic ingredients and cook something simple à la Alice Waters. If I'm feeding a larger group, I want maximum visual impact and abundant food that's easy to eat. Following are some of my favorite nights.

PIZZA MY HEART GAME NIGHT

When I have a bunch of pals over to play Celebrity or charades, I like to buy a stack of inexpensive frozen pizzas imported from Italy (I get mine at Trader Joe's for about $4 each), and dress them with a variety of different toppings before baking. Raw sliced mushrooms and bell peppers, olives, prosciutto, and so on—small amounts of inexpensive veggies and meats can turn a modest pie into something that looks like it came from a restaurant. If I have no toppings on hand, I just drizzle a little extra-virgin olive oil on top of the pizza after it's baked to make it taste expensive. I serve the pizzas with inexpensive red Italian table wine (I like Sangiovese, Chianti, and Montepulciano) and a big green salad, and I make individual ramekins of instant chocolate pudding topped with a squirt of whipped cream for dessert.

GUILTY PLEASURES COCKTAIL HOUR

From Cheetos to SnoBalls, frozen Milky Ways to Cracker Jack, there's a lot of delicious and inexpensive junk food out there. Although I make an effort to avoid processed food in my everyday life, I have nothing against a little toxic indulgence once in a while. And I like a cheap party! For this one, I buy as many empty calories in bulk as possible and arrange them in my prettiest bowls all over my house. I serve orange-soda martinis and milk shakes spiked with rum, and I ask guests to bring a CD of the songs they're most embarrassed to love. Then everybody just hangs around and listens to cheesy music, feeling deliciously guilty.

LOCAL FLAVOR

When I'm feeding just a couple of close friends, I like to go to the farmers' market and pick up some really special meat and produce. Then I serve it in the simplest way possible. Big hits have been broiled lamb chops with lemon, oregano, and olive oil, or free-range chicken and olive stew. I serve whole fruits and maybe a special cheese for dessert. You'll be amazed at the luxurious ingredients you can afford when you limit yourself to serving a couple of perfect items and leave out unnecessary extras. The key is to only buy things in season.

CHAMPERS AND CAV

Even though I'm not the world's biggest fan of caviar, I love the look on people's faces when I serve it—they instantly feel spoiled and indulged. Bought and served carefully, caviar doesn't have to break the bank. First of all, invite guests for a pre-event cocktail hour, not a whole evening at your home, so all you have to buy is snacks and drinks, not dinner. (If your friends are still hungry, everyone can go out to a restaurant together after the main event and split the check.) Second, shop smart. The best way to save money on champagne is not to buy it at all—go for sparkling wine instead. Technically, a wine can only be called "Champagne" when it comes from a certain region in France, but there are excellent sparkling wines crafted all over the world. To get the best value, check out domestic options between $20 and $40. As for caviar, get the best you can for your money. Caviar is simply salted fish roe, usually from sturgeon or salmon, and its price is dictated by the kind of fish it comes from. There are three grades of Russian caviar—Beluga, Osetra, and Sevruga—and Sevruga, the least expensive, is good enough to impress connoisseurs and newbies alike. To care for your caviar, keep it in the coldest part of your refrigerator, and eat it within a week of opening. To make caviar go farthest, serve it garnished with chopped eggs, minced onions, sour cream, and toast points.

PANTRY TIPS & TRICKS

LEFTOVERS

94. Don't throw away leftover sparkling wine or champagne just because it's gone flat—especially if it's expensive! To restore bubbles to wine that has lost its sparkle, just drop a raisin into the bottle. The natural sugars will work magic.

95. Don't toss out cookies that have gone dry—just place them in a jar overnight with a slice of apple. The moisture in the apple will soften them up a bit.

96. Ordinary spaghetti sauce can become Bolognese with some leftover meatloaf crumbled in.

97. Tuna salad easily becomes casserole when combined with noodles, topped with a mixture of bread crumbs, olive oil, and grated Parmesan cheese, and baked.

TRICKS

98. There's nothing more frustrating than over-salting a soup or stew you've spent countless hours—and countless dollars in ingredients—making. Don't throw it down the drain! Try adding some wedges of raw potato or apple to absorb the salt. Let the soup simmer for 10 minutes or so and then remove the wedges. If your soup is still too salty, try sprinkling in a spoonful of sugar. And if that doesn't work, a dash of apple cider vinegar may do the trick. Finally, try diluting with water or low-sodium broth.

99. Soup that's too fatty is just as bad as—or worse than—soup with too much salt. If you have some time, put the pot in the refrigerator, wait 30 minutes, then skim the grease from the top and reheat. If you're short on time, toss in a few ice cubes and remove them as soon as you see grease sticking to them. Or try tossing a large lettuce leaf into the pot and letting it absorb any extra oil. Discard the leaf once it looks limp.

100. When gravy is too greasy and there's no time to cool and skim, whisk in some baking soda, a pinch at a time, to cut the fat. Taste the gravy after each pinch to ensure you don't add too much.

101. How many times have you burned the gravy just as everything else is ready to go to the table? When you don't have enough time—or pan drippings—to start from scratch, stir in 1 teaspoon of smooth peanut butter for every cup of gravy. This should eliminate any burned taste, but be sure to survey your guests about peanut allergies, or you could have a situation much worse than scorched gravy on your hands.

102. Before tossing a pot of coffee that tastes scorched and bitter from being overheated, add a pinch of salt to the pot. The sodium can help make it taste fresh again.

103. If your recipe calls for buttermilk but you don't have any, just add 1 tablespoon of white vinegar or lemon juice to each cup (240 ml) of milk.

104. Yogurt can be substituted for heavy cream in recipes that don't require cooking. But when it's cooked, yogurt can curdle, so try whole milk or half-and-half instead.

105. When a recipe calls for dredging meat in flour, put a small amount of flour in a plastic bag, add the meat, and seal and shake. You'll use much less flour in a bag than you would in a bowl, so your food will be lighter but your flour canister won't.

MAKING THE MOST OF WHAT'S ON THE SHELF

106. Treat your kitchen like a restaurant. Keep an inventory list, and make note of an item when your supply is running low. Then you'll be able to replenish before you run out, and you'll be able to buy in bulk at low prices.

107. When you are shopping for food, pay for nutrition, not marketing. Brand-name sodas, sugary cereals, and gimmicky items with lots of packaging cost much less to produce than to advertise, which means your dollars are going toward media buys rather than high-quality ingredients. Look for products with whole grains and protein, and avoid preservatives. You'll get much more nourishment for your money.

108. Not sure what to do with those crumbs at the bottom of the chip bag or cracker box? Stale snack foods and cereals make excellent coatings for oven-baked meats and veggies—perfect for times when you want a crunch without frying. Just dredge meat or veggies in flour, dip in beaten egg, and then press into a bowl of crushed cereal. Bake at 450°F (200°C/gas 6) until golden brown and cooked through.

109. If you mix some rice into your salt-shaker, the salt won't harden. The rice absorbs condensation that can cause clumps.

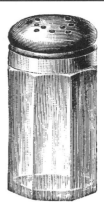

110. Storing your brown sugar in the freezer will keep it from hardening.

111. Believe it or not, honey is the only nonperishable food substance in the world, so don't get rid of it when it crystallizes or takes on a cloudy appearance. Microwave it on medium heat in 30-second increments to make it clear again.

112.
Don't throw away brown sugar when it hardens. Revive it by sealing a slice of fresh bread or an apple in its bag and allowing it to rest overnight. Or try microwaving it at high power for 30 seconds.

DON'T TOSS IT — REINVENT IT

113.
Because plastic storage containers are porous, they retain food odors even after they're washed. Crumpling newspaper inside after washing and drying will absorb the odors and keep containers fresh. Be sure to give them a quick wash and rinse to remove any ink or dust from the newspaper before using again.

114.
Plastic containers also stain easily. Soak them in water for a few minutes before filling, or mist them with a nonstick cooking spray.

115. Turn your clean, used plastic baggies inside out and reuse them before throwing them away. You'll need to buy half as many this way.

116. Use food-storage containers to organize jewelry, craft supplies, and toys, instead of looking for solutions at the organization and storage supply store.

117. Reuse aluminum foil. Just wash it in hot, soapy water and drain in your dish rack.

118. Paper towel rolls make great mailing tubes. Just reinforce them by wrapping them in packing tape. Seal the ends by tracing out circles of cardboard to match their size, and attach those with packing tape as well.

119. Cut up old shower curtain liners to line kitchen drawers. Just wipe them down thoroughly beforehand with antibacterial surface cleaner.

120. Tissue boxes make perfect dispensers for plastic grocery bags.

121. Use old pillowcases to make cute gift-wrap satchels—just tie with a pretty ribbon.

122. Use clothespins to keep chip bags closed, or glue a piece of cheap plastic magnet (the kind businesses advertise on) to a clothespin and use it to fasten a to-do list to the fridge. My favorite so-simple-it's-brilliant use for clothespins, though, is to use them to convert a cheap wire hanger into a pants hanger.

123. Empty Styrofoam egg cartons make excellent ice-cube trays when you need lots of extra ice for a party.

124. Used CDs make excellent coasters for candles or drinks. Just cut felt circles to fit and use a hot-glue gun to fasten them to both sides.

125. Old CD cases bent backward make excellent recipe holders in the kitchen.

126. An old desk organizer finds a new home in the kitchen, keeping cookie sheets upright. You can also use a napkin holder to organize your bills.

127. A piece of chicken wire or chair caning—or an old toothbrush holder—can be slipped inside a vase and used to hold cut flowers in place invisibly.

128. Old straws can be used to elongate flower stems that are too short for a particular vase.

129. Stale, oil-free popcorn works as well as Styrofoam peanuts for keeping fragile items safe in the mail.

130. Nail polish in out-of-fashion colors can be used to code your keys.

131. Old bubble wrap makes a great jewelry roll for travel. Just roll jewelry inside the wrap like a burrito. Use masking tape to attach small pieces.

132. Rolling fabric—a pillowcase, a table-cloth, even a remnant—around mailing tubes will keep the fabric wrinkle free in your suitcase or dresser drawer.

133. Use an old contact lens case to carry a small supply of your pills.

134. Line a pizza box with craft paper and use as an art portfolio.

135. Cut up old greeting cards to make bookmarks.

136. Spray the inside of a mayonnaise jar white and use it to hide valuables in your kitchen cupboard or fridge.

137. No need to panic over a tiny lost item—just slip a nylon stocking over your vacuum cleaner wand and suck away. Be sure to check the end of the wand frequently to see if you've found it.

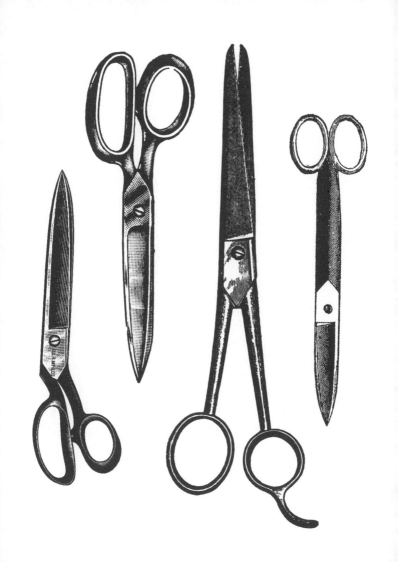

AROUND THE HOUSE

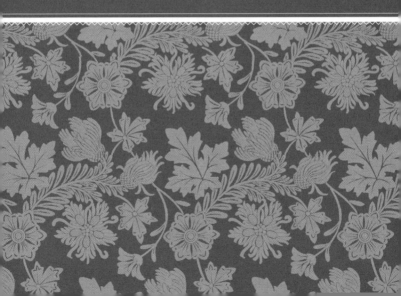

CLEANING

SUPPLIES & SHORTCUTS

138. With cleaning products, the rule of halves almost always applies. Use half a cup of detergent, half a dryer sheet, half a sponge, and so on. You'll effectively cut your supply costs in half, without losing effectiveness.

139. The citric acid in orange instant-drink-mix crystals will clean the inside of your dishwasher just as well as expensive cleansers made specifically for this purpose.

140. Stainless-steel polishes can be pricey. Instead of purchasing them, use a mix of denture cleaner and water.

141. Instead of using exorbitantly priced (and toxic) oven cleaner to absorb a spill, use salt. Pour salt liberally on top of the oven spill to absorb it—make sure you act quickly, before the stain hardens—then use paper towels to remove the mess.

142. Steam clean your microwave without using any cleaning products at all. Just soak a clean dish towel in water, place the towel in the microwave, and "cook" on high for 30 seconds to 1 minute. Remove the towel with tongs—it will be hot!—and use a paper towel or clean rag to wipe down the inside of the microwave.

143. When you're cleaning your garbage disposal, there's no need to invest in a specialized product you'll rarely use. Just freeze a solution of 1 part water and 1 part white vinegar and crush it in your disposal. The vinegar's acid will break down any undigested food and get things moving smoothly. To deodorize, put half an old lemon in the disposal and turn it on.

144. Windshield washer fluid costs less than half the price of brand-name home glass cleaners. Buy it in bulk when it's on sale, and refill your old brand-name spray bottles.

145. Steel wool pads can be tough on oven ware—and they don't come cheap. So forgo them entirely! Baked-on food will come off easily when scrubbed with half a raw potato dipped in powdered detergent.

146. Don't waste cash on sponges and scrub pads when you have mesh onion bags lying around—use them to clean your dishes.

147. Never buy aerosol air fresheners—they're murder on your pocketbook, as well as on the environment. Just squeeze a few drops of fresh lemon juice into your vacuum bag before you run the machine to freshen the air in your home.

148. Minimize your use of paper towels to cut costs. Use rags for most wipe-down tasks.

149. Instead of using a harsh drain cleaner that can harm your pipes, blast clogs with a solution of equal parts baking soda and vinegar. Just mix and pour down the pipe, then flush with hot water until the drain clears.

150. Newspaper cleans glass better than paper towels do—it leaves no residue.

151. Make your own kitchen or bathroom deodorizer by adding 2 teaspoons baking soda to 2 cups (480 ml) water in a spray mister. Add a drop of essential oil—such as tea tree or lavender—to make a scented version. Spray lightly on kitchen and bathroom surfaces.

152. To clean a greasy coating from the inside of your oven, place a bowl of water on the lower oven rack, and a bowl of ammonia on the top oven rack, while the oven is still warm. Leave the bowls in place overnight as the oven cools; then thoroughly wipe the inside of the oven in the morning. All the grease will wipe out easily.

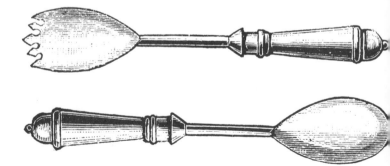

153. To make copper shine, rub it with half a cut lemon dipped in salt, and apply a light film of lemon oil. Or, for a one-step polish, use ketchup. Just apply a thin coat and rub off.

154. A cork will shine your silverware. Just rub it along the surface of knives and spoons—it will pick up whatever is tarnishing the surface.

155. Buff china with baking soda to remove tea stains. Just dip a damp kitchen towel or washcloth in some baking soda; then gently rub the stain in a circular motion. Wipe off with the clean side of the cloth.

156. A solution of 1 part white vinegar and 3 parts warm water will clean crystal without leaving streaks or spots. Just use a sponge to gently bathe crystal in the solution. Air dry upside down.

157. Rubbing alcohol will remove spots from stainless steel. Just apply some to a cotton ball and wipe the tainted spots away.

158. Kitty litter will absorb paint and oil spills in an instant. Dump a liberal amount of kitty litter on top of the spill, and then wait until the spill is absorbed. Gather the whole mess up in sheets of newspaper and sweep up any leftovers.

159. Use a couple of teaspoons of baking soda dissolved in hot water to clean inside thermoses or coffee pots. Just fill the vessel two-thirds full with hot water; then add baking soda, close the lid, and shake. Dump the solution and rinse clean.

160. Soak tarnished silverware in the cooking water left over from boiling potatoes. The starch will dissolve the tarnish.

161. Furniture marks, fingerprints, and food spots will come right off wallpaper when rubbed with stale bread. The bread attracts whatever's on the surface, much like the Magic Eraser products you'll find in the cleaning aisle.

162. Clean varnished wooden surfaces with a cloth dipped in cool, weak tea—it contains no detergent that could break varnish down, and its faint staining property will add luster to the wood.

163. Rub superficial scratches in light wood furniture with brazil-nut or walnut meat. The natural oils in the nut will nourish and seal the damaged wood, so the scratches seem to disappear. Just go down the length of the scratch, rubbing with the nut in small circles. Then polish with a soft cloth.

164. Scratches in mahogany wood will vanish when dabbed with iodine—its natural color makes it the perfect touch-up paint.

165. Remove white spots from mahogany by coating them with petroleum jelly. Leave it on for 48 hours; then wipe off with a soft cloth.

166. A cinnamon stick boiled in water will deodorize the kitchen.

167. Dirty tile grout will clean right up when scrubbed with the rough side of a sponge, or an old toothbrush, dabbed with white toothpaste.

168. Don't throw out old or mis-matched socks. They are perfect for dusting blinds—just slip them on your hand and run across the slats.

169. Black lacquer can be hard to clean—its shiny finish is delicate and scratches easily; plus, any moisture on its surface almost always streaks. Wipe it with a soft cloth soaked in cool, strong, black tea—the tea won't leave a residue or damage the finish.

TEA PARTY

Most of us know that tea contains high concentrations of antioxidants and is a healthful alternative to coffee. But you might be surprised at how many things it's good for outside of a teacup.

• It removes odors from hands and feet. Whether you've been chopping garlic or running a marathon, soaking in tea makes stinky smells a mere memory.

• It's a great pick-me-up for houseplants. Water them with weak tea once a week.

• It soothes sunburn. Apply damp, cold teabags as compresses.

• It makes an excellent air deodorizer. Just put cold, weak tea in a spray bottle and mist in musty rooms. Earl Grey is especially fragrant.

• And guess what else you can do with tea bags? Mend torn nails! Just cut a small swatch out of an unused bag, dot with clear nail polish until it's tacky, and place over the tear. Apply two coats of clear nail polish to seal.

170. Stop yelling at guests who forget to use coasters. A paste of salt and vegetable oil will remove water rings from wooden furniture. Just apply the paste to the rings and massage in with a soft cloth.

171. After just-painted windowsills dry, coat them in furniture wax to make them easy to wipe down and keep them squeaky-clean.

172. Sprinkle baking soda on upholstered surfaces before you vacuum them. This trick also works to deodorize carpets, and it keeps your vacuum cleaner smelling fresh.

173. Save a scorched pan by sprinkling it with baking soda. Add 4 to 5 tablespoons (approximately 60 to 75 g) salt and let it stand overnight. Then scrape out the remains with a rubber spatula.

174. A carpet remnant is the best tool for scrubbing stains off carpet.

LAUNDRY

175. Add some salt to the cycle (at the same time you add the detergent) when washing dark clothes for the first time. This will help set their color. A touch of salt will also brighten clothes that have faded.

176. To restore deep color to black clothing that has faded, add coffee or strong tea to the rinse water. Half a dryer sheet will take away any coffee or tea odor.

177. Who says you need to toss dryer sheets after using them just once? They can actually perform for up to four loads. After the sheet has lost its scent, use it as a dust cloth. It will also work well as a duster when taped to your disposable sweeper mop.

178. Put a clean, dry old towel in the dryer with your wash. It will absorb moisture, helping clothes dry faster.

179. Treating your clothing with respect will make the items last longer and help them keep their shape and vibrancy. The simplest way to ensure that you don't damage clothing during cleaning? Don't remove care labels—and do take the time to read them.

180. Avoid dry cleaning bills. Most items whose care labels read "dry clean only" can actually be washed with care at home. After all, dry cleaning is by no means dry, and avoiding it can actually extend the life of a garment. Here's how to handle a variety of different fabrics:

- Wash silk in a sink full of tepid water with a capful of gentle shampoo. Hang on a sturdy hanger (wooden or cloth, not wire) to dry.

• Wash woolens in lukewarm water—too hot or too cold can shrink or toughen fibers—on your machine's shortest cycle. Dry flat on a towel in the bathtub.

• Wash cashmere in gentle shampoo. Press water out gently and let dry flat on a towel, being sure to shape the garment so it doesn't stretch.

• If velvet is looking tired but doesn't necessarily need to be cleaned, use a soft brush to stroke it in the direction of its nap; then use an iron to steam its underside and hang it up to dry.

• You'd be amazed at what the small brush attachment on your vacuum cleaner can do for a suit. Work it around the collar and lapel and you'll find you need to send the suit to the cleaners much less frequently.

181. To help your washer and dryer kick their sock-eating habit, use a safety pin to connect socks to one another before you wash them.

182. If your favorite sweater shrinks inexplicably, soak it in water with a touch of gentle shampoo, rinse, and reshape.

183. When ribbed cuffs or waistbands lose their elasticity, dip them in hot water and they should spring back together.

184. Can't remove a collar ring on a light-colored shirt? Rub it with a heel of stale bread before washing.

185. A solution of 2 tablespoons cornstarch mixed into 1 pint (480 ml) of cold water makes the perfect spray starch. Keep it in a plastic spray bottle and shake like crazy before using so it stays dissolved. Spray onto a clean clothing item just before ironing. This is great for people who are sensitive to the synthetic fragrance in commercial spray starch.

186. If you're not sure whether new items are colorfast, add 1 teaspoon of Epsom salts for every gallon (3.78 L) of wash water to your washing machine. Since the average washing machine capacity is about 20 gallons (75 L) of water, this means about ½ cup (60 g) Epsom salts for the average load. This will keep colors from running and keep them bright.

187. Another way to brighten colors: add ½ cup (120 ml) vinegar to the rinse cycle.

188. There's no need to spend $10 on a mesh lingerie bag. Wash underclothing in a pillowcase knotted at the top.

189. Disposable dryer sheets are really expensive and create unnecessary waste. To get the benefits of reduced static and added fragrance, moisten a washcloth with inexpensive liquid fabric softener and toss into the dryer with your laundry.

190. To reduce static without using softeners, pop a ball of aluminum foil into the dryer with wet clothes.

191. Forgetting to remove a load from the dryer, only to find it later wrinkled beyond belief, is frustrating. Instead of washing it all again, just throw a wet towel in with the wrinkled stuff, and re-dry. The wet towel will create steam that releases wrinkles.

192. Don't get rid of feather pillows when they flatten out—just throw them in the dryer with three clean tennis balls, and run everything through a low-heat cycle. The balls will beat the feathers back into shape.

193. To maximize drying time, open the dryer halfway through its cycle and remove lightweight items that are already dry—this will help them last longer and reduce the drying time of the rest of the load.

194. If you accidentally scorch a cotton tablecloth, napkin, sheet, or shirt while ironing it, soak the item in cold water overnight. This may help restore the fabric's softness—but unfortunately it won't remove a burn.

195. Wash clothes inside out to prevent pilling on the exterior surface, which is caused by items rubbing against each other during the wash cycle.

196. Don't throw old towels away. Sew them together to make an outdoor blanket, or cut them into cleaning rags so you can save on paper towels.

OUT, DARN SPOT!

I am ashamed to admit how many times I've tossed a perfectly good (and expensive!) garment just because it's tainted with a stubborn stain. Rarely do the highest-tech stain sticks and salves work for me, and I've managed to stump my ingenious dry cleaner on more occasions than I can count. Well, it turns out that acting immediately is the key to successful stain removal, and, further, some of the most effective cleaning agents are already sitting right in your cupboards. Here are some foolproof, low-cost stain solutions that really, truly work:

• Grass stains and dirt come right out when treated with liquid dish soap. Just rub it in—no water necessary—let it sit for a few hours, and launder as usual. If grass stains persist, treat them with white vinegar or hydrogen peroxide.

• Spray yellow underarm stains with hydrogen peroxide. Let them sit for 30 minutes; then toss in the washing machine.

• Blood will usually come right out when you soak it in cool water (never hot—it sets the stain). If the stain is especially stubborn, soak it in hydrogen peroxide for 30 minutes and then wash as usual. You can also make a paste out of meat tenderizer and water to lift the stain.

• Chewing gum will peel right off a garment if you stick it in the freezer for a few hours.

• Remove ink by placing a paper towel underneath the stain and blotting the top with a cotton ball soaked in rubbing alcohol. The towel should absorb the stain. You can also try spraying the ink spot with hair spray and blotting with a clean paper towel.

• Grease and oil stains will usually come right out when treated with shampoo—just make sure not to use a fatty, moisturizing formula.

BATHROOM

197. Porcelain paint is expensive—car paint is much cheaper and just as durable. Repair chipped sinks and tubs with auto touch-up paint, which you can buy in a small brush-pen dispenser at an auto supply or discount store.

198. Quadruple the yield of a roll of toilet paper by pressing it flat before you put it on the bathroom roll. Since it will be harder to unroll because of the creases, you'll use fewer squares.

199. Don't throw your shower curtain away when it's covered in soap scum—just toss it in the washing machine with two bath towels and 1 cup (240 ml) vinegar. Keep an eye on it and take it out before the spin cycle, which could tangle and damage the curtain. (You can wash both fabric and vinyl curtains this way.

200. To unclog a toilet without a plunger, pour 1 cup (240 ml) dish soap into the bowl. Wait 10 minutes and add 1 gallon (3.78 L) of boiling water. After 10 more minutes, the toilet should flush easily.)

201. Before calling a paid professional to consult on a household problem (in the bathroom or elsewhere), go to your local hardware store and pick the shopkeeper's brain. He or she may help you solve the problem yourself. If you do need to hire an expert, at least you'll know just what to expect and be able to avoid unnecessary costs.

GLASSES & DISHWARE

202. To prevent delicate china cups from chipping, hang them from hooks suspended under your cabinets instead of stacking them.

203. Pouring hot liquid into glassware can cause it to crack. Prevent damage by placing a spoon into the glass before you pour—the metal will absorb the heat from the liquid.

204. To keep from breaking crystal glasses when you wash them, place a rubber mat in your kitchen sink.

205. If you chip or nick a piece of good crystal, you don't need to throw it away. Just take it to your local jeweler, who will be able to file the chip smooth.

206. If you're having a dinner party and you don't have enough wineglasses, spare yourself a run to the cookware store, and serve European style: pour wine into your tiniest stemless tumblers for a look that is festive and cool.

207. If you do need to buy glasses for a party, head to a restaurant supply store instead of a department store—you'll save money and you'll score durable, high-quality goods.

FURNITURE

208. Conceal minor furniture scratches with melted crayon wax.

209. Grease stains will come right out of leather when treated with stiffened egg whites. Just beat a couple of egg whites until they form soft peaks, and apply to leather with a soft cloth. Massage the egg whites in gently; then wipe off with a clean part of the cloth.

210. Olive oil will soften dehydrated "crunchy" leather upholstery. Keep leather from flaking by washing it with saddle soap and a damp cloth every couple of months. After it dries, drip some olive oil on a soft cloth and gently polish.

211. Leather that has lost its shine can be revived by a quick wipe-down with a cloth dampened with milk.

212. Rotate and flip your mattress every couple of months to keep it firm and lump free as long as possible.

PEST CONTROL

213. Put away that toxic spray and deter bugs naturally.

• Ants hate honey mixed with boric acid, white pepper, sage, mothballs, chalk lines, baby powder, apples, and cucumbers with salt on them.

• Wasps and hornets hate having their wings coated with hairspray.

• Cockroaches hate boric acid.

• Flying bugs hate smoke. (Use any scented candles— they don't have to be made of citronella.)

• Crawling bugs hate walls and baseboards painted with a solution of 2 tablespoons alum mixed into 3 quarts (2.83 L) boiled water.

• Moths hate cheesecloth bags full of cloves hanging in your closet.

• Mosquitos hate onions and oranges.

DECORATING

SPRUCING UP A ROOM

214. To bring an entirely new look to a room, just rearrange the furniture. Put a chair at a diagonal or move a lamp to a new spot—you'll be amazed at how different things look.

215. When hotels re-model, they often sell barely used, high-quality furniture for a song. Check your local newspaper and online classified ads to find out about sales.

216. Buy cheap, ugly art in frames at yard sales and toss the art. Free frames!

217. Pick up art books for next to nothing at Goodwill, garage sales, or library sidewalk sales; then cut out and frame the images in them. This looks especially sophisticated when you hang associated images in a grid—say, a series of flowers above a bed, or a bunch of black-and-white travel photographs in the kitchen.

218. Look into outdoor furniture, even when you're decorating indoors and especially for playrooms. It's durable and tends to be inexpensive.

219. Make your own bulletin board by buying a painter's canvas at an art-supply store, padding it with cotton batting, and then covering with fabric. Just staple the fabric to the canvas's frame.

220. Use beach towels to re-cover the pillows on indoor-outdoor furniture.

221. Hang paper lanterns as chandeliers.

222. Check online classifieds for incredible deals on furniture—people will sometimes practically pay you to take their stuff when they're moving.

223. Find inexpensive needlepoint pillows at thrift stores. Remove the needlework and frame it, or sew it onto new pillows from a discount store.

224. Glue feathers onto an inexpensive lampshade for a super-spendy decorator look. Just layer the feathers onto the shade so they're overlapping one another—like fish scales—fastening them to the shade with a glue gun.

HOME FRAGRANCE

225. A bowl of charcoal briquettes placed on the floor of your closet will prevent dampness and odors.

226. No need to invest in exorbitant scent sticks or candles—just place a drop of your favorite perfume on lightbulbs before company comes over.

227. Potpourri is easy to make—just dry some orange peel strips and mix them with your favorite sweet spices, like cinnamon sticks and whole cardamom, allspice, or cloves. Leave a few small bowls throughout the house.

228. Sprinkle cinnamon on aluminum foil and place it in a hot oven, leaving the door open. It will smell like you're baking.

229.

Now that we've discovered that breathing candle smoke can be toxic, scent sticks—reeds that diffuse liquid home fragrance from a bottle—are all the rage. At department stores, reed diffusers can cost as much as $100, but you can make your own for less than $5. Just find a glass container with a small opening (about the size of a quarter). Fill it with a mixture that contains 3 parts DPG (dipropylene glycol, a base for fragrances sold in most hardware stores) and 1 part fragrance oil. The fragrance oil is where you can get creative—use any essential oil you like, or blend a few to create a custom scent. The truly industrious can switch scents seasonally—peppermint oil is crisp and fun for winter; lavender works well for spring. You can also use your favorite cologne or eau de toilette—just be sure not to choose anything too strong. Once you've made your mixture, drop in a handful of reeds—skinny sticks of bamboo or rattan that you can buy inexpensively online. The fragrance mixture will be absorbed into the reeds and will subtly scent your room.

KEEPING CUT FLOWERS FRESH

230. A shot of vodka added to a vase will keep your cut flowers fresher much longer than plain water will. A spoonful of sugar and a pinch of lemon juice will also do the trick.

231. Tulips don't just cost money; they also love it—pennies, specifically. Drop a few in their water and they'll last twice as long.

232. Add a few teaspoons of bleach to water in a glass vase to keep it from going cloudy. The bleach won't affect the look or life of the flowers.

233. Spray flower petals with hair spray just before they wilt; this will help prolong their life.

234. If your flowers wilt prematurely, place freshly trimmed ends in hot water for 20 minutes or so; then put them back in their original vase. They should draw the water in and plump up immediately.

WALL, WINDOW & FLOOR MAINTENANCE & DECORATING

235. Before you hang a picture, place a piece of tape on the spot you're going to nail—that way the plaster won't crack, chip, or flake.

236. Before you buy cans of new, custom-blended paint, ask a sales associate at the paint store whether they're selling any returned paint at a discount. Though you may not get the exact color you had in mind, you'll probably be able to find something similar to what you were looking for—at a fraction of the cost.

237. Instead of buying decorator fabric curtains, find large flat sheets in a pattern you like and sew a pocket for a curtain rod on top. Just fold the sheet's top edge over an inch or two (2.5 to 5 cm), depending on the size of your drapery rod, and sew a tunnel. You can even use hemming tape for a no-sew solution.

238. Treating the feet of your furniture with furniture wax will protect wood floors from scratches.

239. Use clear nail polish to repair small tears in your sheer curtains.

ENERGY &
APPLIANCES

SAVING ON ENERGY COSTS

240. Load the dryer while it's still warm from the last load. Your dryer will use less energy, since it doesn't need to heat itself up.

241. Invest in a thermostat with a timer so the heat's on only when you're home.

242. Turn your water heater off when you go out of town.

243. Along the same lines, be sure to turn off all the lights before you leave on a trip.

244. Set your ceiling fan in the correct direction. In summer, run it clockwise to draw hot air up. In winter, run it counterclockwise to push hot air down.

245. Turn your thermostat from 72°F to 68°F (22°C to 20°C) or lower. You'll save as much as 15 percent on your heating bill. Invest in a programmable thermostat to keep the temperature in your home at a minimum level.

246. Nestle a hot-water bottle or two at the foot of your bed instead of turning on central heat at night.

247. Clean your lightbulbs weekly by dusting them with a rag. Dusty bulbs reduce the efficiency of your lighting fixture.

248. Close off unused rooms to lower your heating and cooling costs. Shut their heating vents, and place rolled towels along the crack between the door and the floor to prevent drafts.

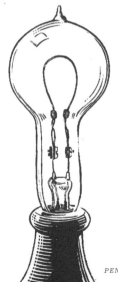

249. Run an extra spin cycle in your washer, especially when washing heavy fabrics like denim and canvas. This will reduce drying time and save energy.

250. You've heard about putting a brick in your toilet tank to cut back on water usage and save money. To save even more, fill a half-gallon milk jug or 2-liter soda bottle with water and place it in the toilet tank. This will cut your toilet water usage in half.

251. Be good to your appliances—from washers to dryers, refrigerators to toaster ovens—and they'll be good to you. Clean them frequently and remove any dust that might clog the works. Vacuum their vents so they can work efficiently. They will cost less money to run, and they'll last longer.

252. Find any air leaks in your home by shining a flashlight along the edges of doors and windows. Have a friend stand on the other side of the window. If your friend sees a ray of light on the other side, there's a draft. You can also close a piece of paper in the door or window and then try to pull it out. If it slips out easily instead of tearing, you've got a leak. Air sealing—treating these gaps with weather stripping or caulking—will dramatically reduce heating and cooling costs. Use caulk for gaps less than ¼ inch (60 mm) wide, and weather stripping for movable joints like windows and doors. You can save up to $30 per year on your heating bill if you add weather stripping just to your front and back doors.

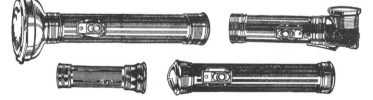

253. Compact fluorescent bulbs last ten times longer than incandescent ones, and they use less electricity—an amount equal to $60—over their lifetime.

254. Put motion sensors on outdoor lights.

255. Electronics consume 40 percent of their energy when they are turned off. Keep them unplugged, or invest in a timed power strip that will shut electronics down when you're not using them.

256. If your water heater was made before 2004, wrap it in insulation and save 10 percent on your water-heating bill.

257. Have your furnace tuned up every other year to get major savings on your heating bills.

258. Use cold water to wash your clothes and save the energy your washer would otherwise use to heat water. Set your dryer on the moisture sensor, not the timer, and cut energy use.

259. Reduce the temperature on your water heater from scalding to just hot—about 120°F (48°C) is plenty warm and will save you money.

260. Install a low-flow shower head and save more than 7,000 gallons (26,498 L) of water a year—$30 to $100.

261. Fix that leaky faucet and save 2,700 gallons (10,221 L) of water per year.

262. Put a drop of food coloring in your toilet tank to test it for leaks. If water in the toilet bowl takes on a tint, you may be wasting up to 200 gallons (759 L) of water a day. In that event, call a plumber to have the leak fixed.

263. Run full loads of clothes and dishes. Most of a dishwasher's energy is used to heat a set amount of water, so running smaller loads wastes both energy and water.

264. To save water, turn off the faucet when brushing your teeth, and take a shower instead of a bath.

265. Install aerators in your faucets. They will reduce flow rates and water consumption, cutting your water bill substantially.

ELECTRONICS, APPLIANCES, GADGETS & COMMUNICATION

266. Computers are like cars—often much cheaper but just as good when you buy them used. When shopping for a new computer, check out the "refurbished" sections of manufacturer Web sites first (Apple and Dell both offer them). Although these deals are rarely publicized, some manufacturers offer factory-reconditioned products—usually from returns—with great warranties and even better savings.

267. Make "phone calls" from your computer. Services like Skype will let you make long-distance—even international—calls at a great savings. Or look into VoIP phone service for your home phone. Companies such as Vonage provide phone service over the Internet instead of phone lines, and the resulting bills are much cheaper.

268. Use video chat instead of the phone—most services are free and it's fun to see whomever you're talking to. Many computers now come with webcams, but if yours doesn't have one, just pick one up for less than $20 at any discount store. You'll recover the $20 in your first month's long-distance telephone savings.

269. Evaluate your landline extras. Services such as caller ID and voicemail can add as much as $50 to your monthly bill, and, since most of us have cell phones these days, you may not need them. In fact, you may not need a landline at all.

270. To save money on supplies, perform as many tasks as you can digitally, instead of using paper.

• Sign up for online bank and credit card statements—not only will the electronic notices help you avoid late fees, but you'll also be able to dispute mysterious charges quickly and manage your budget on your computer with little additional effort.

• Pay your bills online. This will help you save on stamps and checks, and you'll also have a record of your payments when tax time rolls around.

• To save on postage, send an e-mail instead of snail mail.

• Create an electronic holiday card rather than a paper card or newsletter.

• Send invitations online instead of via post. A bonus benefit? RSVP's are much easier to keep track of this way.

271. Instead of buying a fax machine, use an online service to send and receive faxes. Though you'll need a scanner or digital camera to send certain things, such as signatures, you can send documents directly.

272. Go for the slower Internet service option if your service provider offers a choice. A change in surfing speed is often barely perceptible, but the savings can run from $10 to $25 per month when you downgrade.

273. Never spring for the extended warranty at electronics stores. The manufacturer's warranty usually offers enough coverage.

274. Use open-source software whenever you can. You'll save on licensing fees. Most brand-name word processing, photo organizing, and video editing programs have a free, open-source equivalent—sort of like store-brand cereal or generic drugs. To find open-source programs that suit your needs, check out www.osalt.com.

275. Connect all electronic devices to a surge protector—this will prevent power surges that can damage them.

276. When your favorite CD gets scratched, try rubbing toothpaste into the CD's surface with a soft cloth—some toothpastes will make scratched CDs stop skipping.

277. Look for unusual, expensive appliances at moving, garage, or yard sales. You may find a $200 bread machine for $20, simply because someone can't bear to pack it up and move it.

LIFESTYLE

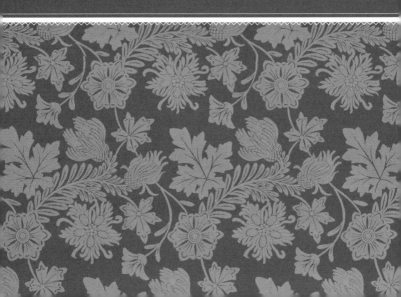

BEAUTY & WARDROBE

COSMETICS

278. Spa foot massages are expensive, and family members never seem to want to give them without asking for one in return. To give your own feet a treat, fill a 2-liter soda bottle with warm water and roll it back and forth under the soles of your feet.

279. With aftershave costing as much as $10 per ounce, you can save hundreds per year by making your own. Actually, there's nothing to "make"—just splash white vinegar onto freshly shaved skin. Any worries you have about the smell will vanish as it evaporates, and your skin will be cool and free of bumps.

280. Many catalogs sell extra-absorbent hair towels that promise to wick moisture from just-washed mops in a fraction of the time that terrycloth would take. You can find the same moisture-wicking material in the car-care section of your favorite discount store, for a fraction of the price—just look for the microfiber cloths that are made for drying cars.

281. Silicone frizz-control products are really expensive, and those tiny containers run out quickly. Instead, try working a few drops of extra-light olive oil into your hair when it's damp. Extra-light is a better choice than extra-virgin, because it has no smell and is the least-expensive grade. Avoid getting the oil on the roots of hair, where it can create a greasy appearance—apply it to dry ends instead. Add a few drops of lavender essential oil for a clean, outdoorsy scent.

282. To get a much higher yield from powdered beauty products such as baby powder or translucent face powder, cover half the shaker holes with paper or tape. This will help you control the amount of powder you remove from the container. This is also a good trick for other powdered scrubs you use in the kitchen.

283. Dry shampoo is enjoying a retro resurgence—it creates texture and "cleans" hair without water. Instead of shelling out $20 or more for a salon brand, just sprinkle baby powder into your roots and brush (obviously, this works better on paler hair shades than darker ones). Some people have concerns about the health risks of inhaling the talc in baby powder, so if you're worried about holding your breath, stick to the dry shampoo.

284. Buy a pump top for your shampoo and conditioner bottles, and ask everyone in your household to use just one pump. You'll go through less than half of what you usually use. This also eliminates the hassle of fumbling with slippery bottles in the shower.

285. Flat soda water makes an excellent setting lotion. Just spray it on damp hair, and blow dry or set in Velcro rollers. Beer supposedly works just as well, but the smell could pose a problem, unless you're going out to the pubs and are of legal drinking age.

286. Old tights make excellent hair bands — just snip off the toes and then snip what will seem like an infinite number of donut-shaped elastics off each leg.

287. Seal in your signature scent by applying a thin layer of petroleum jelly on top of it on your skin. This will keep fragrance from evaporating. Use just a small amount of petroleum jelly, however; you don't want it to rub off on clothes.

288. Do you know that magical spray the ladies in the nail salon mist your toes with to get them dry and shiny fast? It's nothing more than baby oil. You can create the same effect at home by brushing a coat of baby oil over just-polished fingers and toes — this will also help prevent chipping.

289. Cosmetic counters at high-end department stores usually offer unadvertised complimentary samples of their products so potential new customers can try them out. If you are intrigued by an expensive skin-care item, ask a sales associate if you can take some home to see how your skin reacts to it before you invest.

290. Clean out your old lipstick tubes—stick them in the dishwasher upside down, or clean them with a cotton swab soaked in rubbing alcohol—and use them as purse-sized pill boxes.

291. Diluting your shampoo by as much as half will not reduce its efficacy, especially if you lather, rinse, and repeat—which most hairstylists say is not necessary either! It's perfectly fine to lather and rinse once.

292. Before you toss out dehydrated mascara, nuke it to see whether its moisture level can be restored. Remove the mascara's brush cap and cover the tube with a damp napkin. Place it upright in the microwave—you can prop it up in a cup if it won't stand on its own—and "cook" it on high for 10 seconds. Replace the wand and pull it out again—the bristles should be moist and evenly coated.

293. Just like clothes dryers, hair dryers will work better and last longer if de-linted with diligence. Remove any debris from the screen at the back of your hair dryer with an old, dry toothbrush—or vacuum it with a small brush attachment.

294. Pamper yourself at a beauty school instead of a spa. Beauty schools offer everything from massages to haircuts at a fraction of the price, and instructors monitor trainees so nothing goes awry.

295. Find out if your favorite luxury salon has a training night, when assistants learn cutting and color skills from master stylists. You can get a high-end style for next-to-nothing.

296. Say yes when the lady in the department store offers you a free makeover—especially before a special event. Just be sure to ask first whether any fee is required. Instead of making an appointment with a pricey professional makeup artist, call ahead to make an appointment at a department store counter. While this service usually does carry a fee, it's almost always redeemable in products—for example, if the makeup lesson costs $100, you'll go home with $100 in products.

297. Buy makeup at a big-box discount store instead of a department store. Many high-end brands are creating affordable self-service lines, and some discount stores even offer department-store-style testers. Most important, cosmetics are almost always returnable for cash or credit, even after you've opened them—just be sure to check the rules on your receipt.

298. Use pure muslin or plush cotton washcloths instead of buffing or peeling creams to exfoliate your face. These are reusable, less likely to irritate (as long as you use a hypoallergenic laundry detergent and hot water when washing them), and just as effective at giving skin that gorgeous glow.

CLOTHING CARE

299. Remove pills from sweaters, wraps, and dresses by "shaving" them with a clean electric razor. This process can make something totally shabby look new.

300. If you don't have an electric shaver, try gently buffing a pilly sweater with a pumice stone.

301. Before you replace a stuck zipper or throw the item away entirely, rub the zipper's teeth with a bar of soap to lubricate them. If that fails, mist the zipper with spray starch to get it moving again.

302. A rip in an unlined raincoat can be hard to mend. Instead of sewing it together, close the tear with a strip of transparent adhesive tape on the inside of the coat. You'll be surprised by how well it sticks.

303. Padded hangers are expensive but necessary to help knit items maintain their shape. Make your own by removing shoulder pads from dated tops and sweaters and sewing or fabric-gluing them to wire or wooden hangers.

304. If you or someone else in your life is hard on shirt buttons, dot some clear nail polish on the thread fastening the button to the shirt. This will strengthen the bond and help keep the buttons from popping off. Just be careful not to get any of the nail polish on the shirt, and give it plenty of time to dry.

SHOES

305. Toothpaste, when brushed onto leather shoes with a soft cloth, will remove scuffs, and it will also remove tar from soles. Make sure the toothpaste contains no bleaching agents such as peroxide, or it could affect your shoes' color.

306. Shoe polish doesn't work on patent leather. To maximize luster, clean it with milk.

307. Suede doesn't do well with shoe polish either. To remove scuffs and stains from suede, polish them with fine-grade sandpaper.

308. You don't need any special material to polish shoes. Use old pantyhose.

309. Rub soaking-wet leather shoes with saddle soap to keep them from cracking or drying in a strange or uncomfortable shape.

310. High heels can get nicked easily—especially by sod or subway grates. To camouflage spots where leather has pulled away from the heel's base, use auto paint.

311. Shine leather shoes with vegetable oil.

ACCESSORIES

312. To shine up an old straw hat, spray it with hair spray.

313. You can also spray the toes of your pantyhose with hair spray to keep them from running. (And you already know that clear nail polish will stop a run in its tracks.)

314. Rubbing beeswax on the toes and heels of tights and stockings will also keep them from snagging.

315. Putting lotion on your feet, legs, and hands before pulling on hosiery will make it less likely to snag on dry bits.

316. Soak your hosiery in cold water spiked with vinegar instead of detergent. This can help prevent odors and pulls.

317. Mysteriously, pantyhose and tights seem to last longer when stored in a plastic bag in the freezer.

JEWELRY

318. Chlorinated water can damage or discolor gold jewelry. Take your baubles off before you jump in the pool or hot tub.

319. Another place not to wear your favorite necklace: the hair salon. Chemicals in hair color can react with precious metals and ruin their finish forever.

320. Untangle a delicate chain by coating it with butter or vegetable oil.

321. Use small chunks of pencil eraser to temporarily replace lost earring backs.

322. Don't spend a lot of money using fancy jewelry cleaners. Dish soap works just as well.

WELLNESS

REMEDIES

323. Plantar warts hurt. A lot. Not to mention that the traditional method for removing them—applying strong acid to dry the skin out and then slicing off layers with a razor blade—is difficult and expensive. Some people say a banana peel poultice works just as well. Tape a banana peel on top of the wart before bedtime, and the wart may disappear in a few days.

324. If your doctor prescribes expensive medications, don't be shy about asking for samples. Pharmaceutical companies provide doctors with plenty of samples in the hope that they'll prescribe their brand-name medications to patients. At the same time, most pharmacies will offer you the option to fill your prescription with generic drugs instead of brand-name ones, if generics are available. This is usually a great cost-saving option, but check with your doctor to make sure there are no substantive differences between the brand-name and generic versions.

325. Squishy cold packs are hard to find—you usually have to seek them out at a medical supply store—and very pricey. Make your own by mixing 3 parts water and 1 part rubbing alcohol and pouring the mixture into a zip-top plastic bag. Even when frozen, the mixture will stay viscous and flexible, and the bags can be refrozen a limitless number of times.

326. A spoonful of honey works as well as most lozenges to soothe a sore throat.

327. There's no need to buy a special cream when you get a sunburn—soothe a burn with a cloth soaked in apple cider vinegar or witch hazel. Or try cooling skin with cold, wet peppermint- or chamomile-tea bags. For extra comfort while you sleep, sprinkle sheets with cornstarch before you slide in so your raw skin doesn't rub against the fabric.

328. To keep athlete's foot at bay, soak feet in white vinegar.

329. A paste of baking soda and water will relieve the inflammation that results from bug bites.

330. To soothe a stomachache, dissolve 2 teaspoons cinnamon in a cup of warm water and drink.

SPORTS & FITNESS

331. Some players say that tennis balls will bounce again if stored in a gas oven overnight. There's no need to turn the oven on—the pilot light will provide enough heat to restore the bounciness. You can also try putting them in the microwave on high for 30 seconds.

332. Coating white canvas tennis shoes with spray starch before you wear them for the first time will help them resist stains and stay white.

333. Once they're dirty, clean canvas sneakers with shaving cream or carpet shampoo. Spread the product over the shoe's surface, scrub with a nail brush, wipe with a damp rag, and let dry.

334. Your baseball glove will stay free of cracks and keep its shape when stored with a ball in its palm.

335. Top-of-the-line sports items—from golf clubs to tennis rackets—are often little better than those a couple of grades lower. Before making a big purchase, talk to a pro or consult online review forums for guidance about which model will give you the highest quality for your money.

336. When it comes to athletic shoes, find your brand, model, and size and stick to them. This way, you can stock up when shoes go on sale, whether online or at department or sporting goods stores.

337. Join a free training group for a cause. Get in shape without joining a gym, and contribute to your favorite foundation or non-profit at the same time, by signing up for a charity run, swim, or bike race. Check with your local cancer society or heart disease research organization for a list of resources.

338. Check bulletin boards at local sporting goods stores for free running groups and yoga classes.

339. Don't be snobby about where you exercise—your local YMCA or community center probably offers the same classes and equipment as a fancy health club, at less than half the price.

340. Buy health club memberships at the end of the month, or the end of the year, when salespeople are striving to meet their quotas. This is when you'll be able to bargain for the best discount. Ask for the initiation fee to be waived, or for a free month, free guest passes, or personal training sessions.

341. Cancel any memberships you haven't used in over two months. If you find later that you miss one, you can ask if they will let you reinstate your membership; some clubs will permit you to rejoin if it hasn't been too long.

342. Avoid injuries. Obviously, this advice is even better for your body than it is for your wallet, but, from ice packs to physical therapy, the cost of sports injuries can really add up. Stretching before and after exercise—perhaps using a yoga strap, foam roller, or exercise ball—can greatly reduce your risk of getting hurt. Consult a health pro or exercise trainer for specifics.

343. Rather than spending money on exercise DVDs, borrow them from the library or consult a "virtual" trainer online.

344. Rather than paying for weight-loss support, join an online community and participate in the message boards and chat rooms. Someone will usually be available to speak to you around the clock, at no cost.

345. Play golf during the week, when fees are lower, instead of on the weekend, during high demand periods.

LIFESTYLE

PERSONAL FINANCE

LOWERING BILLS

346. Pay someone to do your taxes for you. Most people will save at least the cost of tax preparation when they consult an expert— probably much more.

347. Don't use out-of-network ATMs. An extra $3 to $5 per week can add up to about $250 per year—just to withdraw your own money.

348. Ask your credit card company to lower your annual percentage rate. Agents on the toll-free line may be authorized to reward good customers with rate reductions, and shaving off just a couple of percentage points can save you hundreds of dollars a year.

349. Consolidate your student loans.

350. Contest any and all credit card and bank fees if you think they're unreasonable—customer service agents are allowed to reverse these at their discretion.

351. It may seem like pie in the sky, but check with your state's department of unclaimed funds to see whether you're due any money.

352. Buy all your insurance—homeowner's, renter's, life, car—from the same company, and save hundreds of dollars per year.

353. Property and renter's insurance requires a record of all your possessions—but many of us never get around to making one until it's too late. Don't worry about getting detailed photos and written documentation—just walk through the house with a video camera and explain what you see. Keep a copy stored on your computer, and give a copy to a friend to store on his or her computer in case of fire or theft.

354. Pay insurance bills annually instead of monthly. This will save you money in finance charges.

355. Discuss increasing your insurance deductibles. This can seriously lower your premiums.

356. If you purchase something consistently every month, whether it's a series of yoga classes or a morning latte, find out if prepaying for multiples will get you a discount.

357. If you're interested in trading stocks and bonds, consider using a self-service online account instead of a broker. You'll save a mint in fees and have tight control over and access to your funds.

HOME OFFICE

358. Don't throw stamps away when they stick to each other. Soaking them in water will separate them but it also destroys the adhesive, so try popping them in the freezer for a couple of hours instead.

359. If your stamp has lost its stickiness, lick the envelope's adhesive strip and rub the back of the stamp over it.

360. Use both sides of the paper when writing notes or printing documents. This may seem obvious, but you'll use half as much!

361. Even if you're no longer a student, shop for supplies at back-to-school sales during late summer and early fall.

362. Ask at your local stationery store for any supplies they plan to throw away—from orphaned greeting card envelopes to incomplete marker sets. And always check damaged goods sections for big discounts.

363. Buy economy-sized printer cartridges. You'll get much more printing for your buck.

364. Choose a printer that allows you to replace one cartridge color at a time. This way, when you run out of black, you won't need to throw away one hundred pages' worth of red.

CAR MAINTENANCE

365. Few people know you can reuse antifreeze—indefinitely.

366. Clean out your trunk. Drop off that stuff you've been meaning to take to the Salvation Army; move those golf clubs into the garage. The lighter your car, the less gas you use.

367. Before replacing your air filter, check with your car dealership or your mechanic to see whether it's washable. If it is, just gently scrub it with warm water and detergent and it'll be almost as good as new.

368. Proper tire pressure is essential for maximizing your car's mileage. Check your tire pressure at least once a month to save on gas consumption.

369. Have you ever been approached by an entrepreneur in a parking lot offering to fix the dents in your car? The "technology" employed by these people is usually nothing more than a bathroom plunger and some touch-up paint. If you have these items, there's no reason you can't try sucking out the damage yourself before heading to the body shop.

370. If you're too nervous to try removing the dent with a plunger, try rubbing dry ice over it—many pros say this works. Just be sure to wear protective gloves so your hands don't get freezer burn.

371. Since your tires experience different levels of wear and friction depending on where they're placed on your car, rotate them every 5,000 to 10,000 miles (8,000 to 16,000 kilometers) to maximize their life span.

372. Car-wash shops charge extra to wash the underbody of your car—not to mention the fact that they often knock something loose that can cost a lot to fix. Avoid unnecessary charges and repairs by driving your car over a lawn sprinkler on high pressure.

373. Make your own windshield washing solution with 2 quarts (1.82 liters) rubbing alcohol, 2 cups (480 ml) of water, and 1 teaspoon of liquid dishwashing detergent. This solution won't freeze no matter how cold it is outside.

374. When you're driving in stop-and-go traffic at a slow to moderate speed, open your windows to cool the car instead of firing up the air conditioner. But when you're driving fast on the freeway, using the A/C consumes less fuel than opening the windows—the wind can provide resistance that forces the engine to gobble up more gas.

375. Parking in the shade in the summer saves more than the skin on your bottom. A high car temperature can cause gas to evaporate.

376. Antistatic fabric softener sheets are good for more than laundry. Stash a couple in your car's seat-back pockets for a subtle, invisible air freshener.

377. Obeying the speed limit won't just save you money on speeding tickets— it'll save you gas money, too. According to the U.S. Department of Energy, you pay about a quarter more per gallon of gas for each 5 miles (8 kilometers) per hour you drive over 60 (96 kilometers).

378. Tread lightly on both your gas and brake pedals—this will improve your mileage.

379. Turn your engine off when you're parked. Idling uses gas but takes you nowhere.

380. When your car's door lock is frozen on a winter morning, there's no need to call a cab—or a locksmith. Just hold a lighted match near your key for a few seconds to warm it, and the key will slide right in.

381. The price of gas can vary widely from station to station—even at stations across the street from one another. Thanks to modern technology, though, you can easily find Web sites that will tell you the best price for gas in your area by searching online for "best gas price zip code."

382. Buy gas when the sun doesn't shine. Gas molecules expand as temperature rises, so you'll get more gas for your money when it's cool outside.

383. Use cruise control on highway trips. Keeping your speed consistent will save you money by lowering your gas consumption.

384. If you can avoid driving at rush hour, do. Driving in fits and starts is a sure-fire way to burn through gas.

385. Take a cue from long-haul truck drivers when you're driving a long distance. Cars may seem to flit back and forth from lane to lane, but big rigs lumber along at a steady pace in order to maximize cost and time—just like the tortoise and the hare.

386. Check and replace air filters regularly. Clogged filters can cause up to a 10 percent increase in fuel consumption.

387. That adage about a new car losing half its value the moment it's driven off the sales lot is pretty much true. When you're in the market for a "new" car, opt for one that's barely used instead. Manufacturer-certified used cars have excellent warranties and service plans, and many come off corporate leases, which usually means they were well cared for.

388. When you're looking to buy a late-model used car, check with rental agencies. They often unload excess inventory for less than dealerships will.

389. Buy a car online to get the best price, since dealers compete nationally. Even though you'll likely end up buying your car from a local dealer, they'll have to offer a price comparable to a dealer in a less expensive market.

FUN & LEISURE

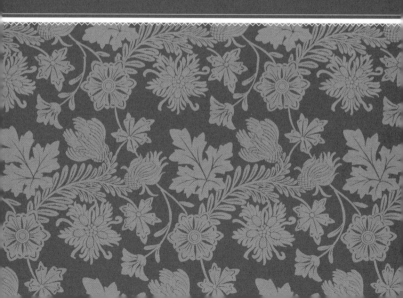

ENTERTAINMENT

OUT & ABOUT

390. If you live near a college campus, attend music and theater events there instead of at a commercial theater. Ticket prices will be lower, and the quality of performance may be higher because of the academic setting.

391. Avoid purchasing season passes and festival tickets—which offer multiple events or screenings at a discount—unless you are 100 percent positive you will be able to use all of them. These packages are like gift cards—most people never use their full value.

392. On the other hand, look into museum memberships. You will often recover their cost in just a couple of visits, and they are often tax deductible.

393. Find out whether your local museum has a free or pay-what-you-can night.

394. Check your local city magazine for gallery openings. Attending the opening night of an art show affords you the opportunity to meet the artist, network with other people interested in the local art scene, and partake in some free wine and cheese.

395. You should also join any free clubs you're interested in, even if only to receive a schedule of programs and activities they offer.

396. See matinees instead of nighttime movies, and smuggle in your own snacks. If you have kids, pop each of them a small bag of microwave popcorn and hide juice boxes in your coat pockets.

PENNY SAVING HOUSEHOLD HELPER

397. Join your local movie theater's loyalty program. You'll earn free tickets and snacks.

398. Buy books online. You'll most likely be able to find everything you want, either new or used—at a steep discount.

399. Resell old books you don't want anymore, either online or at your local used bookshop.

400. Make use of discounts you've already earned. Many clubs and associations, from AAA to your local public radio station, offer significant deals to members. Check their Web sites to see what you're entitled to.

401. Consider scaling back your cable package. Keep track of which channels you actually watch over the course of a week; then evaluate which ones are worth paying for.

402. See if your cable company offers phone and Internet service. Buying all three connections from the same company can often save you lots of money.

403. Join a music, movie, or book exchange club and swap titles with other members through the mail for free.

404. Check with your local theater to see if they offer rush tickets. Some theaters will release, at a deep discount, unsold tickets to those who show up an hour before a performance; many theaters will offer rush tickets only to students and seniors, but some may offer the tickets to any interested buyers. A bonus? They're often the best seats in the house, held until the bitter end in order to accommodate VIPs who might show up.

405. Volunteer at a performing arts venue whose programming you enjoy. Ushering a couple of nights per month, or working a few hours in the office sealing envelopes or answering phones, may entitle you to free tickets.

406. Never pay full price for magazines. Discounted subscriptions are readily available online and can save you up to 90 percent off the cover price.

407. Read the newspaper online instead of paying to have it delivered, or restrict your delivery to weekends.

408. If you work for a big company, consult your employee handbook or Web site to see what discounts and freebies you may be entitled to. Your corporation may have affiliations, from museums to theaters to ballparks, that entitle you to special treatment. The same goes if you have a connection to a large university.

EATING OUT

409. Instead of going out to dinner, go out to lunch. Regardless of whether you visit an ethnic buffet or a bastion of fine dining, a midday meal out will cost you much less than a nighttime one would. Beware, though, of weekend brunches—prices will often be jacked up to take advantage of tourists and diners celebrating special occasions.

410. Have dessert at home. Do you really need to pay $9 for a piece of cake when you could get a pint of really good ice cream, or a few bakery cupcakes, for half as much?

411. If you insist on eating dessert out, leave the restaurant and walk to a nearby bakery, yogurt stand, or gelateria.

412. Order sides. A couple of side items— instead of an entrée—make a great meal. You'll save money, and calories too.

413. Explore traditional ethnic restaurants instead of trendy ones. Authentic is almost always tastier—and cheaper—than fusion.

414. Ask whether half portions are available, even if they're not on the menu. Smaller portions will save you money and calories, and they'll probably be just the right amount of food to fill you up, not the huge portions served by many restaurants.

415. Find out if your local culinary academy has a student-staffed restaurant. You'll get super-gourmet meals at cafeteria prices.

416. If you're organizing a group outing to a pricey restaurant, call ahead to see whether the manager can offer a reduced-price prix fixe meal.

417. Choose between appetizers and drinks, and share a dessert, instead of going wild on all courses.

418. Take advantage of happy hour—even if you don't drink—for the discounted appetizers.

419. Take your leftovers home. Even if the only thing that remains from your Chinese dinner is rice, you'll be glad the next day to have an easy side dish to warm up or repurpose.

SHOPPING

420. Pay cash. Research shows that people spend less when they use cash than they do when they use a credit card.

421. Be efficient. Do all your errands at once to save on transportation costs and time, and plan your route so you don't backtrack.

422. Record what you pay each time you buy a staple—toilet paper, tube socks, your particular favorite brand of shampoo. Bring this record with you when you're shopping so you know when a "sale" price really represents a good value.

423. Avoid anything disposable.

424. Never go to the supermarket hungry.

425. Be open to trying new brands or products in order to maximize savings, but if you know you only like one kind of item, don't

try a new kind just to save a few bucks. You might end up throwing the whole thing out and needing to buy a new one.

426. Look into joining a food co-op or produce delivery service.

427. Get to know salespeople at stores you frequent so they're on your side. They'll be more likely to tell you about sales in advance.

428. Shop online for groceries, cosmetics, books—anything you don't need to try on—in order to avoid impulse buys.

429. Never store your credit card information on any retail Web site. This makes it far too easy to buy things without thinking.

430. If you know what you need from a particular store, call to make sure the item is in stock before you make the trip. Not only will this save you time but it will also prevent you from buying other items to compensate for the one you really wanted but weren't able to buy.

431. Don't wait until the last minute to buy an outfit for a special event—feeling under the gun in the fitting room can cause you to spend hundreds of dollars you don't have.

432. Prices on bulk items can be misleading. Just because you found it at a discount warehouse or supermarket doesn't mean it's cheap. Look for unit pricing to see whether you're getting a good value. Divide the price of a package by the number of units it contains—such as rolls of toilet paper, pounds of coffee—to see what it really costs.

433. Keep the inventory in your home stable. Shop for staples before you need them so you're not forced to buy them at an exorbitant price.

434. If you're attracted to a product's packaging, be doubly skeptical about what's inside. A large percentage of an item's cost goes to packaging and marketing.

435. Don't space out while you check out. Checkers make mistakes, and bar codes are sometimes programmed incorrectly. It's your responsibility to ensure you're paying the right amount for what you buy.

436. Use your debit card when you're shopping at big-box stores. Paying with an electronic method will enable the store to track your purchase should you need to return it—even if you lose your receipt.

437. Make a list every time you go shopping—and stick to it. This will help you think of shopping as a goal-oriented activity, not open-ended entertainment.

438. Join sample-sale Web sites. They offer designer fashions for up to 90 percent off retail price.

439. Shop off-season. Buy your swimsuits in early fall, and your winter coats in early spring. You'll end up spending half as much—or you'll be able to buy twice as much.

440. Buy basics in multiples when stores offer a promotion. From T-shirts to bras, from socks to sweaters, buying a few of something you really like can help you save in the moment and stock up for the future.

441. Don't get seduced by outlet malls. Just because a store calls itself an outlet doesn't mean its prices are low or that its goods are top quality. In fact, many outlet versions of big-name stores produce second-rate products just for their outlets, so you're better off buying top quality on sale in their regular stores.

AN INSIDER'S GUIDE TO SAVING ON FASHION

Something I learned while working in the magazine industry is that the most fashionable women in the world never pay full price for the clothes and accessories they wear. When you see photos of editors, actresses, and socialites bedecked in the  newest styles of the season, you can bet that they scored their clothes and accessories direct from the designer, or at an insider's discount. So what are the rest of us supposed to do? Here are some tricks I gathered while striving to dress like a movie star on an assistant's salary. Ten years later, I still use all of them.

• Shop at the end of the season, when one collection goes on sale to make room for the next. I cannot stress the importance of this tip enough. Unless you pose for a living, you do not need to be decked out in the most current styles the moment they appear in stores. By waiting to buy them, you'll get massive savings and you'll be more likely to avoid trendy items whose appeal won't last. To get the inside scoop on sales at department stores and your favorite designer boutiques, ask a sales associate to put your contact information on their preferred customer list. You'll get sale notices before the public, and a salesperson may even offer to keep an eye on the price of your favorite items and call you when they go down.

• Shop sample sales and sample-sale Web sites. Designers often unload their out-of-season goods to "jobbers" who liquidate everything at a fraction of its original price. To find sample sales in your area, do an Internet search.

• Exercise your right to a fair price—keep your receipts. If you buy something at full price, only to see it go on sale soon afterward, bring your receipt to customer service and ask for a price adjustment. You may receive the difference between the original and sale price in cash, in store credit, or as a credit returned to your card.

• Consider opening a credit account at your favorite store. As long as you pay it off every month, a store charge can save you money through incentives, promotions, and bonus points.

• Sign up for promotional e-mails at your favorite stores and Web sites.

• Check online coupon sites for friends-and-family discounts throughout the year.

• Check auction sites for designer items.

• Consider visiting consignment shops for big-ticket appliances and home furnishings.

• Look into Web sites that allow you to borrow designer items for a week or a month.

ARTS & CRAFTS

442. Instead of buying yarn for knitting, unravel your old, unwanted sweaters for free high-quality yarn.

443. Rework old clothes into quilts.

444. Felt old sweaters to make pillows, mittens, or stuffed animals. Sweaters used for felting should be 100 percent wool. Stick the sweater in the washing machine and put it through the hottest cycle with just a little bit of detergent, and dry it on the highest heat in the dryer. When it comes out, it will have shrunk significantly, and it can be cut without fraying.

KIDS

445. When your kids are outgrowing their toys and games, don't throw them away and replace them with store-bought toys. Instead, host a toy swap. Kids can be so fickle about their toys—obsessed with them one day, totally disenchanted the next. Invite friends and family to drop their kids' castoffs at your house, and then set up a toy "shop" in your garage or yard. Brainstorm with other parents to create a currency system, and decide how kids can earn toy bucks leading up to the event. Then, armed with their hard-earned cash, kids can go shopping. This party also works well with teenage girls and clothes, or teenage boys and video games.

446. If you're lucky enough to have a gifted team athlete in your family, try to get him or her sponsored by a sporting-goods company in order to snag reduced-price—or even

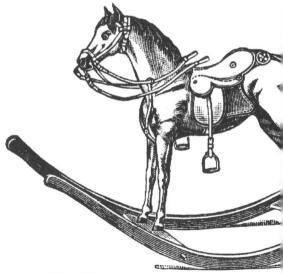

free—equipment. Your child's coach may be willing to call the company rep on your behalf, since the rest of the team may benefit as well.

447. Share a babysitter with friends or neighbors. You don't have to spend the evening together to split child-care costs—just designate one house as the Romper Room and let the kids play with their friends while you go out.

448. Start a babysitting co-op—a rotating play group where parents take one another's kids on a schedule. If you volunteer to babysit a group of children one night a month, you may earn the right to three nights out with free childcare.

449. Consider using cloth diapers instead of disposable ones. Though subscribing to a diaper service will run you about the same cost as using throwaways, washing your own cloth diapers can cost just a tenth of what disposables do.

450. Trade baby wipes for wet washcloths, which you'll wash with a little bleach on your washer's hottest setting.

451. Call companies that manufacture baby products—their toll-free numbers usually appear on their packaging—and ask to be sent free samples of everything from baby powder to powdered formula. They will likely be thrilled to make your family part of their word-of-mouth marketing campaign, if they have one going.

452. Breast-feeding is the single simplest way to save money when you have a new baby. Not having to buy formula can save you more than $1,000 in the first six months of your baby's life.

453. When your little ones outgrow their footie pajamas, simply cut off the feet. If they insist on keeping their toes covered, sew on a pair of loose-fitting socks, or just put socks on them before bedtime.

454. Save kid-oriented fast-food boxes and refill them with homemade food and a trinket from the dollar store—if your kids are young enough, they won't know the difference.

455. Set up a hand-me-down tree with your friends and family. Yearly trades—in person, or through the mail—will get your child many of the things he or she needs and will cost you next to nothing.

456. When your child is preparing an oral presentation, cut leftover paper plates into rectangles to make great index cards in a pinch.

457. A zip-top plastic bag makes a perfect temporary pencil case.

458. Never buy paper lunch bags—they're used once and then thrown away. Instead, get your child a lunch box he or she will enjoy, or repurpose bags or containers you find around the house.

<u>GARDENING</u>

459. Store your garden tools in dry sand to keep them from rusting.

460. Convert your lawn into a garden. It's cheaper to maintain, and the fruits and veggies it produces will save you money on food shopping.

461. Soot and sawdust make great fertilizer.

462. Resurrect a sad houseplant by dousing it with "eggshell tea"—water that has been fortified with eggshells for 24 hours.

463. Garlic cloves placed in soil will work just as well as store-bought pesticides to keep bugs away.

464. Worms will be deterred by matches stuck into the dirt, sulfur-end down.

465. Don't throw away seeds you've had for a while—test their viability instead. Drop them into a bowl of water overnight. Those that rise to the surface will not grow, but those that sink will.

466. White vinegar sprayed directly on most weeds will kill them.

467. Don't just water your lawn blindly—test its moisture level to see when watering is necessary. You shouldn't need to water for more than about an hour per week. If blades of grass pop right back up after you step on them, then the lawn is well hydrated and you can hold off another day.

468. Water your plants early in the morning, before the sun has a chance to cause evaporation. You'll end up using much less water this way.

469. If you can stand to let your grass grow a bit longer, you'll need to water it less frequently. You'll also save time mowing!

470. Look into installing a drip irrigation system in your garden. These can use half as much water as sprinklers.

471. Gray water is nonindustrial wastewater produced during domestic activities such as laundry and bathing, and some people use it to water their lawns and houseplants. Since opinions vary on whether using reclaimed water improves the condition of plants or worsens it, give the process a try and see for yourself.

472.

Homemade compost is better for your garden than any store-bought fertilizer—and it's totally free. Just start an organic waste bin in your kitchen—make sure it's airtight—and toss all your plant-based kitchen waste into it, from banana peels to peach pits. Then, bring the whole mess out to the garden compost pit every day. You can employ worms—they're easy to find at any natural foods store—or Bokashi, a mixture of grain products, to convert the food waste into compost. Then use it to enrich your soil and improve the health of anything you're growing—and keep food out of landfills.

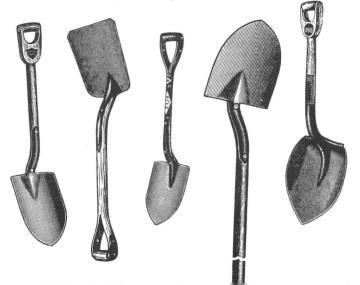

TRAVEL DEALS

473. If you're planning a weekend getaway, try booking a luxurious hotel that caters specifically to business-people. Because they may struggle to meet capacity when work isn't in session, you're likely to score an amazing deal.

474. Travel to Europe during the off-season: between September and May. Because kids are in school, days are shorter, and temperatures can be chilly, there isn't as high a demand for international travel during these months. You will save significantly on airfare and hotels. Added bonuses: you can enjoy ballet, opera, and symphony performances during the regular season, instead of the abbreviated tourist one. You'll be able to get better restaurant reservations. And you'll spend your vacation surrounded by locals, rather than scores of other Americans.

475. Take advantage of local resources. Check the Web sites of the chamber of commerce, any local tourist agencies, and local newspapers at your destination to score insider deals.

Independently owned businesses often post valuable coupons.

476. Consider booking a package through an agency instead of paying for airfare, hotel, and car separately. Because agencies negotiate these rates for groups, you'll pay a group rate even when you're traveling solo.

477. Bring snacks from home on road trips and pack your lunch for a flight—that way you won't pay exorbitant prices for crummy airline or fast food. Just remember—when you're flying you'll be forced to toss any liquids when you go through the security checkpoint, so bring an empty thermos or bottle and fill it at the water fountain.

478. If you book your hotel through a central reservation number—usually identifiable by an 800 or 888 area code—look up the number for the individual location where you'll be staying and ask to be connected to the front desk. Agents at the property are often authorized to offer deals that call-center employees don't know about, so ask them to bring up your reservation record, and then inquire whether you've gotten the best deal going. You may want to ask, "Are you offering any specials?" or "Would it be possible to request a room upgrade?" Or, how about saying, "I heard you're running some promotions—can you give me the details on those?" (It's okay to fib if you haven't actually heard about any promotions.) Even if the desk attendant can't promise you anything until you arrive, you might snag some savings, a better room— or perhaps a basket of fruit.

479. While bed-and-breakfasts often seem cheaper than four-star hotel chains, they don't do the sales volume necessary to allow them to advertise major discounts. Before you commit to a bed-and-breakfast or an inn, be sure to investigate big hotels in the same area. You can

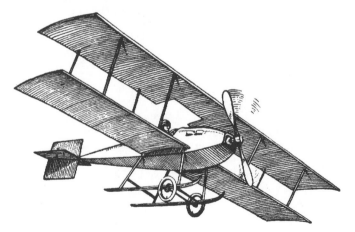

always use the hotel price quoted as a negotiating tool to get the smaller place to come down in price. For example, say, "I've had to book at [insert big hotel name here] in order to stick to my budget, but I've heard your place really offers a special experience. Is there any way you can meet the rate I've been quoted?"

480. Look into doing a house or apartment swap. Many Web sites allow travelers to post photos of where they live and request to trade quarters with people who want to travel to their area. The result? Free lodging, and a much more authentic experience, especially when traveling abroad.

481. Being spontaneous has its advantages— booking travel at the last minute can save you tons of money. Just search "last-minute travel" online and you'll find sites auctioning off flights, cruises, and hotel rooms for a fraction of their regular prices.

482. When renting a car or booking a hotel, be sure to show your auto club membership. This will often earn you at least 10 percent savings.

483. Always check individual rental-car Web sites as well as search engines. They may be offering exclusive deals.

484. See if there are any independently owned rental car agencies in your destination cities. Sometimes they offer better deals than big chains.

485. Find out if your company or university offers any special travel discounts.

486. If you have a major credit card, opt out of rental car insurance. Most credit cards protect you against liability and damage, so the extra $10 to $20 a day in supplementary coverage costs is wasted. If you're not sure what your credit card company provides, call the toll-free number on the back of it.

487. If you're traveling to Europe, check out government-owned hotels and hostels.

488. If you're considering a resort vacation, check out luxury campsites instead. Many provide all the amenities of a great hotel, with breathtaking scenery and outdoor activities, for a fraction of the price.

HOLIDAYS

PREPARATION

489. Shop for holiday cards after the holiday is over, and stockpile them. Themes change very little from year to year.

490. Reuse Christmas cards that have been sent to you as postcards or gift tags. Just cut off the personalized part and glue them into a scrapbook.

491. Send electronic gift cards instead of presents.

492. Never pay a mailing store franchise to pack your gifts for shipping. Pack them yourself with materials you already have around the house.

493. Send packages out early to avoid higher rush shipping rates.

494. Make a base for a holiday wreath with wire hangers. Then just weave decorative items in and out.

495. Popcorn and cranberry garlands are traditional for a reason—they are pretty, and cheap!

ALTERNATIVES

496. Be inventive when it comes to wrapping paper—you can make newspaper, butcher paper, and even paper bags look attractive with ribbons, glitter, and paint.

GIFT-WRAPPING TIPS

I'm the type who's always scrambling to wrap the gift fifteen minutes before the party—and I don't have a gift-wrap room, closet, or drawer to run to in a pinch. And, honestly, for this I am glad. I find mass-produced wrapping paper to be totally uninspired, not to mention overpriced—so I prefer to dress my presents up with stuff I have around the house. It's essentially free, and people really appreciate the care I take to personalize their gifts.

• Any paper can be wrapping paper. Leftover wallpaper is luxe. Butcher paper—in brown or white—can be decorated with stamps or potato prints. You can turn the recipient's name—or any holiday greeting—into a fun pattern by typing it out in a word processing application and repeating it over and over on a piece of printer paper. Newspaper funnies make adorable wrapping for children's gifts. Even kitchen parchment looks elegant wrapped around a small box.

• Instead of using ribbon, tie your packages up with kitchen twine, yarn, or raffia.

• Sew a little satchel out of a leftover garment or piece of fabric, and tie it up with a ribbon.

• Ask a cigar shop if they have any extra boxes they're planning to toss.

• At liquor stores, inquire about empty champagne boxes.

497. Instead of buying a present for each and every one of your friends and relatives, start a white elephant party tradition in your family or workplace. Each person brings one wrapped gift to the event—the host establishes a spending limit beforehand—and then each guest draws a number out of a hat. The guest who draws number 1 chooses a package from the gift pile and opens it. Then Number 2 has a choice—he or she can either open a package or "steal" Number 1's gift. This goes on until all the gifts have been chosen, with the person drawing the highest number getting the greatest range of choices.

THROW A RE-GIFTING PARTY

No matter how much everybody scales back over the holidays, we're all bound to receive a couple of gifts for which we have no use. Instead of letting them languish in a shopping bag at the bottom of your closet until next year, throw a re-gifting party in January!

Ask your guests to come armed with a rewrapped re-gift, then run the event like the white elephant party I mentioned earlier. Draw numbers to decide the order in which guests will select presents, and then everyone can eat and drink as they negotiate and bargain. That massive, strong-scented candle that makes you sneeze just thinking of it? It may be just what your neighbor's been looking for!

Serve repurposed food and drinks to fit the theme of the party—yes, leftovers are just fine! You can even encourage your guests to bring unfinished bottles of wine, cakes, etc. And any gifts that don't get chosen will be received with gratitude at your local hospital or women's and children's shelter—just rewrap them.

498. Instead of Christmas cards, send letters, postcards, or, even better, create an e-mail newsletter.

499. If you do want to print Christmas cards, order them from an institutional printer geared toward business customers—you'll find many options online—instead of a consumer photo site.

500. Instead of gifts, give donations to non-profits in the names of your friends and relatives—you'll receive a tax deduction.

INDEX

n

o

p

r

s

ACKNOWLEDGEMENTS

WHO KNEW I HAD SUCH THRIFTY PALS? FOR PROVIDING ME WITH INGENIOUS TIPS—WHETHER CONSCIOUSLY OR NOT—AND FOR TESTING OUT MY ZANY IDEAS, I OWE THANKS TO BETONY TOHT, MERRITT LEAR, JOE CASSIDY, JUDE ANGELINI, KAREN AND LIZ SILVERSTEIN, MICHELLE DIETZ, CATE AND AARON MILLER, MOLLY FAST, SUSANNAH LESCHER, STACI MARENGO, TUERE MERRIOUNS, LISA CONGDON, KARA CORRIDAN, ALISON MARKOVITZ, WESLEY MORRIS, IKE DELORENZO, MARTHA MCCULLY, DAN DILIBERTO, MATT SURMAN, DANA HOEY, JULIE ROSEFSKY, ELISA ALBERT, STEPHEN FITZPATRICK, AND JEFF BOEHM. SORRY FOR BEING SUCH A NOSY SNOOP AND MAKING YOU ALL TURN YOUR EGGS UPSIDE DOWN. THANKS TO THE BRILLIANT JODI WARSHAW FOR BELIEVING THAT THERE WAS HOPE FOR A LESS-THAN-CAREFUL SPENDER, AND TO ANDY McNICOL FOR FINDING ME THE MEANS TO SUPPORT MY (NOW REFORMED) SHOPPING HABITS. TO MY BROTHER PAUL, FOR BEING THE BEST PENNY (AND HUNDRED) SAVER I KNOW, AND TO MY PARENTS, LINDA AND FRED KNAUER AND JOSEPH DILIBERTO, FOR TEACHING ME TO SPEND LIKE THERE'S NO TOMORROW. FOR BETTER OR WORSE, AS WE ALL KNOW—THERE IS.